Time to Sign with Chi

Table of Contents

Time to Sign inc.

Introduction

TIME TO SIGN, INC.'S MISSION

Time to Sign, Inc. is dedicated to supporting effective and meaningful communication for children, families, caregivers, and businesses by teaching American Sign Language in a fun and educational way.

GOALS

To teach American Sign Language (ASL) to children, families, caregivers, and childcare providers through the use of songs, games, stories, and play.

And

To enhance communication and raise communication awareness in the workplace; to serve as a benefit to corporations, their staff and families; and to enhance their service to the public through the instruction of ASL.

SUMMARY

This Learning Guide is designed to give childcare providers a variety of tools to use in the classroom to teach children American Sign Language (ASL). This book includes theory and research on the benefits of signing with children, information about ASL and other forms of manual communication, language developmental milestones, age appropriate signs and activities, over 200 illustrations of signs, information about playing to learn, traditional and new songs, and references and resources.

Other accompanying products you may wish to purchase is the Time to Sign with Infant/Toddler Music Guide and CD, Time to sign with Toddler/Preschool Music Guide and CD, Time to Sign with Preschool/School Age Music Guide and CD. Time to Sign Infant/Toddler Music Guide illustrates 16 songs in sign, the Time to Sign Toddler/Preschool Music Guide illustrates 18 songs in sign and the Time to Sign Preschool/School Age Music Guide illustrates 20 songs in sign. Learning by the use of songs is the best way for your children to enhance their signing vocabulary. The music guides and CDs are rhythmically paced for children to sign and sing along.

Time to Sign, Inc. conducts workshops and classes for children, families, and childcare providers that compliment the materials contained in this learning guide. We hope you enjoy learning and teaching ASL to your children. For information, comments or questions regarding these materials please contact us at *1(321) 723-6997* or visit our website at www.timetosign.com.

Benefits of Signing with Children

- 2-sided brain activity that increases brain functioning
    - Visual right brain usage
    - Cognitive second language left brain usage
    - Creates additional connections or synapses in the brain
    - Can create higher IQ levels in children
- Enhances fine motor coordination
- Learning a second language makes additional language learning easier
- Raises communication awareness and abilities
- Enhances children's vocabulary
- Babies can communicate their pre-verbal wants and needs
- A fun activity for child and parent/caregiver that reduces frustration and enhances bond between child and parent/caregiver
- Enhances children's confidence and self-esteem
- Enhances reading skills
- Enables children to control their hyperactive tendencies

Classroom Benefits

- Lowers children's noise levels in the classroom
- Reduces need for teachers to raise their voice
- Enables class to support special needs children
- Children pay better attention, they have to look directly at you
- Sign language gets their attention better than the spoken word
- Increased ability to express themselves reduces instances of misbehavior
- Provides children the ability to express emotions
- Increases children's use of manners

Why Sign with Hearing Children?

DR. MARILYN DANIELS BIOGRAPHY

Dr. Marilyn Daniels is a Penn State Professor of Speech Communication who publishes books and articles concerning the use of American Sign Language with both hearing and Deaf individuals. Her book, Benedictine Roots in the Development in Deaf Education, Listening with the Heart, earned wide acclaim in both the hearing world and the Deaf community. Dr. Daniel's abiding interest is the art of human communication in all its forms. Currently she maintains a focus on improving communication by enhancing literacy. To this end she has designed and conducted numerous research studies in which hearing children from babyhood to through sixth grade use various amounts of sign language to enhance their literacy. Over the past ten years Dr. Daniels amazing results from these endeavors consistently demonstrate sign facilitates children's ability to communicate with words.

Dr. Daniels has secured her position as the world's foremost authority on the use of sign language with hearing children with Bergin and Garvey's 2001 publication of her latest book, Dancing with Words, Signing for Hearing Children's Literacy. The major thesis of her book is the value ASL offers to hearing children's literacy. Using sign with hearing children helps them see words, feel words, spell words, acquire words, understand words, speak words, read words, and communicate with words. Sign has also been shown to reduce conflict, increase self-esteem, and facilitate an understanding of human emotions. Dr. Daniels recent findings clearly indicate this bilingual approach with hearing children activates brain growth and development.

DR. MARILYN DANIELS OFFERS SOME THOUGHTS ABOUT SIGNING

Does this sound familiar? You have a crying baby in your arms. She's Pointing to... what? A teething ring? Rejected. The spoon on the counter? No. The crying escalates. Ah, you think, as you offer every single item in the room, if only they could communicate.

Nowadays it is possible to do just that. You can teach your baby to communicate through sign language. Far from simply reducing frustration in the pre-verbal child, itself not a negligible goal, teaching children sign language has additional benefits. Namely increasing their spoken vocabularies, helping them with reading, and improving their linguistic ability in general.

I and researchers in other fields, including psychology, human development, and family science, have independently produced studies demonstrating that infants as young as nine months can learn basic signs, allowing them to communicate with their parents and care givers long before they are verbal. This in turn can reduce parental and infant frustration and help develop a child's self-esteem.

A recent e-mail I received from a former colleague illustrates the point:

> *"Marilyn, I have always been interested in your research regarding teaching sign language to young children. I thought you might be interested to know that in a small way your work has had a neat impact on my family... here's the story. My eldest daughter, Karen, was a communication major at Penn State and attended many Speech Communication Association of Pennsylvania meetings while she was a student. She heard of your work at one of the meetings and she and I discussed it over the years.*
>
> *Karen is now the mother of Emma who is 15 months old. Emma has been able to tell us for about 5 months that she is hungry, wants a drink, wants more of something, and that she is tired because Karen used signs to express those ideas. Em is now trying language - Mom, Dad, shoe, puppy - and still uses her signs to more fully and accurately tell us what she wants. Em also seems to have a true sense of what words are all about and seems to purposefully attempt to attach sounds to concepts. Karen and her husband, Ed, are terrific parents but it seems to my very biased eye that the signing really has helped bypass much of the parent/child frustration that can occur when a child can't get mom or dad to understand their needs.*

I know this is a tiny adaptation of your scholarly life-work but I thought you might enjoy knowing this. We also find that strangers are fascinated by seeing this little person using her signs to get a drink or another bite of food. So, thanks to you for helping us make our Emma all that much more special.

Elaine"

In a way this is not all new. For many years, we have all shown babies how to wave "bye-bye" and demonstrate "so big", and many educators now belief that sign predated speech in the evolution of human communication. This premise has recently been brought to our attention by the posthumous publication of Dr. William Stokoe's last major work: Language in Hand: Why Sign Came Before Speech, published by Gallaudet University Press in 2001. It is significant that Stokoe, the researcher who is credited with legitimizing American Sign Language (ASL) as a bona fide language, makes this claim in the book, which has been referred to as his intellectual will and testament to the field of study that he started forty years ago.

During the past 15 years I, as well as other researchers, have been focused on systematic efforts to use sign language with children in much the same way we use spoken language with them. We have spawned a new movement: teaching hearing babies and children to use sign language. I have found, as my colleague Elaine describes, sign offers parents and caregivers a unique opportunity to communicate in an effortless way with babies and young children. Further, my research shows hearing children who used sign in their pre kindergarten and kindergarten classes scored better on vocabulary tests and attained higher reading levels than their non-signing peers. The studies of others in this country and the United Kingdom are confirming my results.

Here's why the system works. Babies can learn sign language because they understand symbolic communication before they can form words with their mouths. If you stop to think about it, you will realize that children understand their parents long before their parents understand them. Deaf babies babble with their fingers just as hearing babies babble with their voices, but Deaf children are able to sign months before hearing children can speak. This occurs because they have the motor control to make the signs. The vocal apparatus to form speech develops more slowly than the manual dexterity to form signs.

Using sign language encourages language-delayed and shy children to increase their language acquisition skills in a relatively pressure-free manner. It is difficult for some children to speak well, but with sign the children are on a more level playing field and don't feel inhibited. In addition, children are more attentive simply because they have to be. When you are speaking to someone you don't really have to make eye contact, but when you're using sign language, you naturally and unconsciously focus your attention on the person signing. This improves the quality of the communication.

The added benefits of signing derive in part from its unique status as both a visual and kinetic language. There are individual memory stores for each language a person

knows, even at the initial stages of acquiring the second or third language. You intake sign with your eyes, using the right side of the brain. Then like any other language, sign is processed and stored in the brain's left hemisphere. This operation creates more synapses in the brain, adding to its growth and development. It also helps to establish two memory stores in the left hemisphere for language, one for English (or the native language) and one for ASL. So children who use both develop a built-in redundancy of memory, storing the same word in two formats in two places.

Furthermore, because visual cues are taken in with the right side of the brain while language engages the left using ASL activates both sides of the brain at once. In the same way that bilingual children develop greater brain function, users of sign language build more connections or synapses in the brain than those who use English alone and because of the kinetic component of sign language, the ASL brain benefits even more than the bilingual one because of the dual-hemisphere work. Babies using sign language are simply building more brain.

For a more in-depth analysis of this topic I suggest you consult my web site marilyndaniels.com or my book, Dancing with Words, Signing for Hearing Children's Literacy, where you will find additional information. I wish each of you and the children with whom you communicate much success in realizing the benefits of sign language.

Dr. Marilyn Daniels
Marilyn Daniels, Ph.D.
Associate Professor
Department of Speech Communication
Penn State University
120 Ridge View Drive
Dunmore, PA 18512-1699
Office 570 963-2670
FAX 570 963-2535
Mail to:mxd34@psu.edu

American Sign Language (ASL) and Alternative Forms of Communication

American Sign Language (ASL)

What is ASL?

- ASL is a language, used in the U.S. and Canada, that uses no voice. It has its own grammar and language structure (or syntax), including: facial grammatical markers, spatial linguistic information, finger spelling, and individual signs.
- ASL is a true and natural language where the sign often mimics the experiences with ideas or objects.
- ASL is NOT derived from any spoken language. It is not based on the English language or any other voiced language.

SIX BASIC COMPONENTS OF ASL:

- Eye Contact – when signing one looks directly at the individual they are communicating with.
- Facial Expressions – Impact the meaning of signs.
- Body Language – Impacts meaning of signs.
- Mouth Movements – say the word when signing.
- Hand Movements – the dominant and reference hands are used together to create a visual picture of the meaning of the sign.
- Signing Space – an imaginary window of space between the upper torso and in front of the face where most signs are done.

All six basic components are essential for fluent ASL conversation!

Alternative Forms of Communication

SIGNING ESSENTIAL ENGLISH (SEE1)

Uses ASL hand signs together with the grammar and syntax rules of spoken Standard English. It is very literal and uses strict English word order. Every article, verb and verb part (e.g., "am & going"), conjunction, preposition, etc., is signed.

SIGNING EXACT ENGLISH (SEE2)

Uses ASL hand signs together with the grammar and syntax rules of spoken Standard English. It is very literal and uses English word order. There are only minor differences between SEE1 and SEE2 (e.g., compound words have a different, single sign in SEE2 – SEE1 uses the two separate signs for each word part of the compound word: bedroom).

SIGNED ENGLISH

Similar to SEE1 and SEE2, however it uses ASL signs in a more simple, "concept" delivery. Not all words are signed. It does use English word order, but far less "structure." Primarily intended for use with young children and others with limited cognitive skills.

CUED SPEECH

Uses set of hand shapes (not formal ASL signs) that "add value" to speech-reading. The hand shapes are made at specific locations around the face to help distinguish different sounds that look similar on the lips.

PIDGIN SIGNED ENGLISH

The form in which most hearing people sign to deaf people. PSE is using ASL signs but in English word order. Most interpreters translate in PSE.

Three Channels of Communication

1. Body Language (Crossed arms, Eye contact, Smiles, Etc.)
2. Tone & Modulation (Emotion, Volume, Tone, Etc.)
3. Words (Spoken, Written, Listened, Read)

VERBAL COMMUNICATION:

- Effectively combining the three channels improves communication.

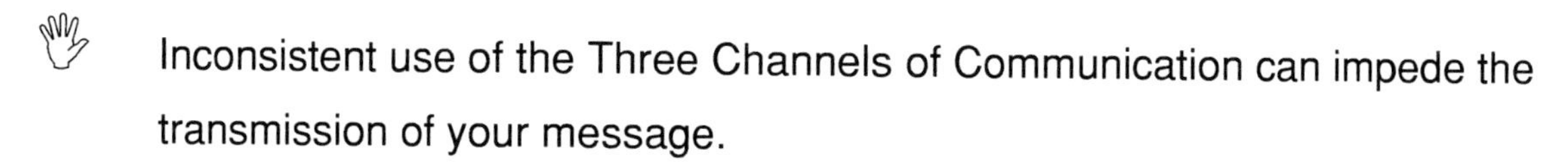

- Inconsistent use of the Three Channels of Communication can impede the transmission of your message.

Listening Skills and Communication Hints

EMPATHIC LISTENING

- Is to identify with and/or understand the person you are listening to emotionally and intellectually.

BENEFITS

- Empathic listening enables us to better understand others' frame of reference.
- Empathic listening fosters meaningful communication and creates close relationships.
- Empathic listening invites the speaker to tell their story and release their feelings.

WHEN USING EMPATHIC LISTENING YOU HEAR/SEE...

- ...what the other person says
- ...understand what others really mean.
- ...the ideas the speaker is conveying.
- ...what people think is important.

WHEN USING EMPATHIC LISTENING YOU...

- ...are aware of non-verbal communication.
- ...use appropriate tone & modulation.
- ...select the correct words to communicate.
- ...are able to listen to, and comprehend, the speaker's frame of reference.

COMMUNICATION HINTS

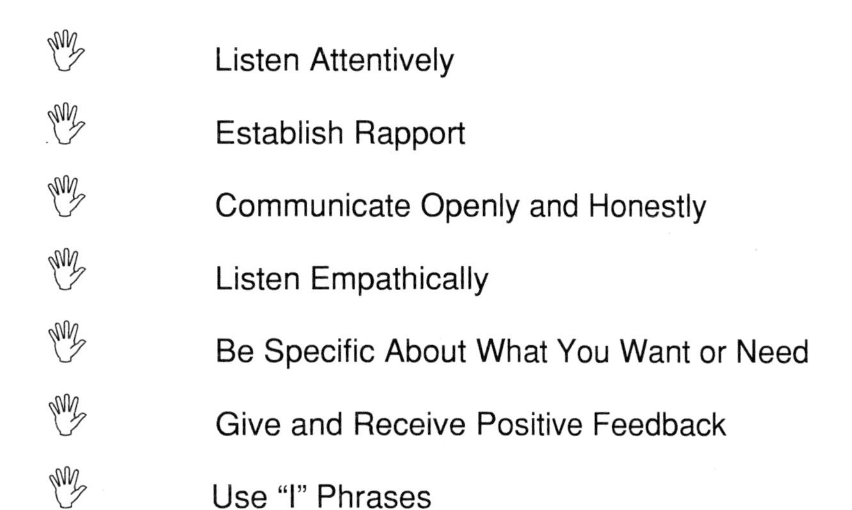

- Listen Attentively
- Establish Rapport
- Communicate Openly and Honestly
- Listen Empathically
- Be Specific About What You Want or Need
- Give and Receive Positive Feedback
- Use "I" Phrases

Signing with Children

WHEN DO I START SIGNING WITH MY CHILD?

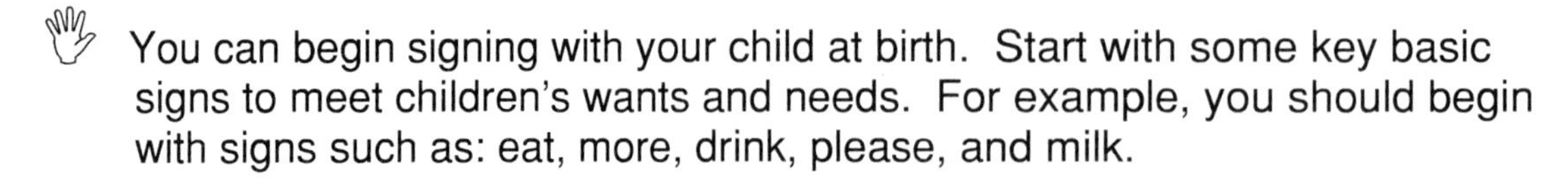

- You can begin signing with your child at birth. Start with some key basic signs to meet children's wants and needs. For example, you should begin with signs such as: eat, more, drink, please, and milk.

- Begin with one or two signs then work your way up to a few more. Don't be discouraged if your child seemingly doesn't notice your signs. Be consistent! One day the children will simply produce their first signs.

- As you see the children begin to use their first few signs regularly, begin introducing additional signs. Be sure to observe children's cues, and practice introducing signs slowly, clearly, and in context.

- Children learn best when everyone who is caring for them uses the same signs the same way. "Mixed-message" signs can frustrate children. Repetition and consistency are the key factors for children's learning.

WHEN ARE CHILDREN READY TO SIGN?

- When children attain enough motor coordination they will begin to respond.

- When children have been exposed to a sign on a daily basis and have had time to practice processing it's meaning.
- When children demonstrate an active desire to communicate – pointing, vocalizing with tone & modulation (babbling or jabbering sounds; conversational or inquisitive), grunting while pointing at object/person, and other attempts at physical or visual cues to get attention or to enlist assistance.

WHEN IS THE BEST TIME TO TEACH A SIGN?

- **"Quiet Alert" State** – Infants in this state provide a lot of pleasure and positive feedback for caregivers. It is the best time to provide infants with stimulation and learning opportunities. In this state children will display the following characteristics:
    - Minimal body activity
    - Brightening and widening of eyes
    - Faces have bright, shining, sparkling looks
    - Regular breathing pattern
    - Curious about their environment, focusing attention on any stimuli that are present

- **In context** –Children are perpetually ***"in the moment."*** For learning to occur, it must be connected or associated to a current event. For example, just prior to offering more milk (bottle or nursing), use the signs for "more milk." Repeated, consistent use of a sign in context will allow children to begin making the connection on their own. Then they will try to imitate the sign themselves. Eventually, they'll respond to your signs for "more milk" by gesturing or signing "yes" or "no."

- **Eye "Gaze" Contact** – Use these opportunities to focus children's attention on some person/object/event ***and*** you at the same time, wait a moment, introduce (or repeat) a sign, say the word while signing it at the sight line between you and the child. This provides the "context" to "associate" learning and "make meaning."

GAZES

- ***Expressive Gaze*:** Children look at you to communicate wants, needs, thoughts, or feelings.
- ***Chance Mutual Gaze*:** Children's eyes and your eyes meet without intent or particular reason.
- ***Pointed Gaze*:** Some event or sound causes a child and you to first look in the same direction for its source (person/thing/event) – Next, you both turn and look at each other.

INCORPORATING AMERICAN SIGN LANGUAGE INTO YOUR DAILY ROUTINE

- Learn the signs for some of the traditional songs that you sing with your children.
- Use common signs with infants, particularly during feeding times to help them learn to communicate while they are pre-verbal. Words such as eat, milk, more, drink, hurt, cold, and hot are easy to sign and particularly useful for the pre-verbal child.
- Sign the alphabet.
- Sign the numbers throughout the day (circle time, head counts, lunch counts).
- Sign the names of the foods at mealtimes.
- Teach children to sign the colors and encourage them to use both the sign and the word when naming colors.
- Teach the children to fingerspell their names.

- Teach the children signs for common actions: eat, play, sing, jump, walk and dance.
- Reduce aggression in your classroom by teaching children signs for emotions and manner signs, and signs for common words that they can use if they get frustrated or angry such as: no, stop, mine, and help. This will reduce the noise level in the classroom as well.
- Teach the children how to sign the names of animals that you discuss in your classroom.
- Use the signs for words commonly used during daily interactions with children such as: mommy, daddy, work, home.
- Teach the children to sign "potty" when they need to use the restroom. This will help to reduce the number of interruptions you experience during the day.
- Teachers can use non-verbal cues such a "no" or "stop" across the classroom without having to raise their voices or interrupt a conversation.

THINGS TO KNOW PRIOR TO SIGNING

1. Dominant Hand – use to refer to begin and make the sign(s). Use your normally dominant hand as your dominant hand in sign language. If the sign is a one-handed sign then you use your dominant hand to form the handshape. If you are left- handed then you use your left hand as your dominant signing hand. In this text, the right hand is the dominant hand.
2. Reference Hand – use to support your dominant hand in making the sign(s). In this text, the left hand is the reference hand.
3. Negative Modifier – shake your head "no" as you produce the sign.
4. Gender Signs – male signs are formed in the forehead area, while female signs are formed in the chin area.
5. Facial Expressions – should support what you are signing. "Your face will surely show it."
6. I Love You Sign – combines the letters I, L, and Y.
7. Person Indicator – "er". Both hands just inside the shoulder, palms facing each other, hands coming down simultaneously from the shoulders to the waist.

Birth to 6 Months

DEVELOPMENTAL MILESTONES

- Crying is primary form of communication
- Responds to sound
- Vocalizes sounds – gurgling and cooing
- Follows objects
- Smiles and laughs
- Recognizes faces and scents
- Coos when you talk to them
- Prefers human faces to all other patterns and colors
- Can distinguish between bold colors
- Amuses themselves by playing with hands and feet
- Turns toward sounds and voices
- Imitates sounds, blows bubbles
- Squeals
- Recognizes own name

SIGNS

milk	up	hear
more	finish/all gone	mother
eat/food	water	father
diaper change	bottle	baby

baby – criatura, bebé

Place the dominant hand in the crook of the reference hand and make a gentle rocking motion from side to side.

As if cradling a baby in your arms.

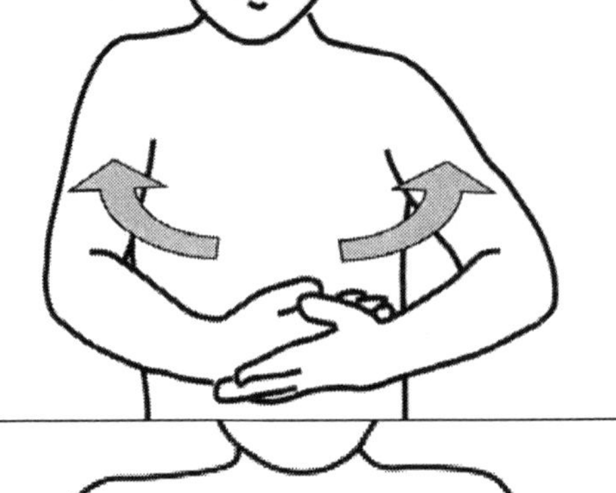

bottle - botella

The reference open hand is held palm up. The dominant "C" hand moves from on the reference hand up. As if holding a bottle in your hands.

[also: cup, glass]

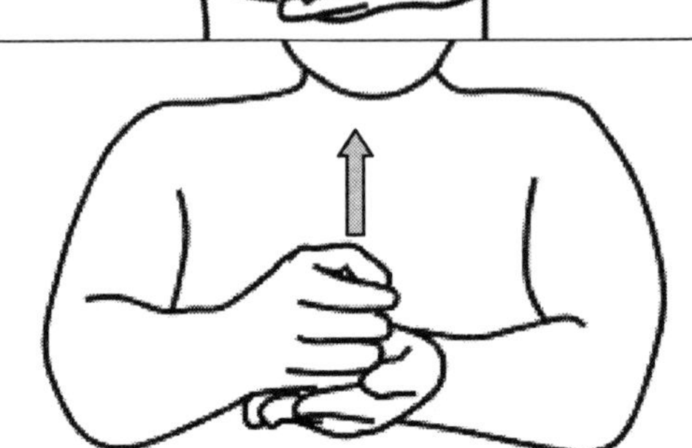

change - cambio

With both modified "X" hands, place the dominant "X" so the palm faces forward, with the reference "X" facing it. Twist the hands around until they have reversed positions.

[also: adjust, adapt]

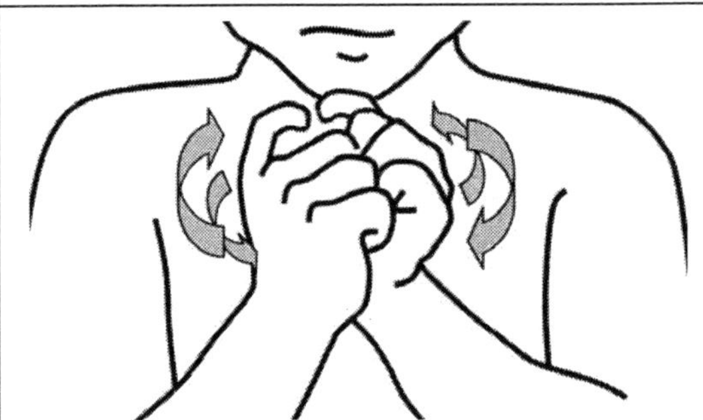

eat - comer

With the thumb and fingertips together, palm facing down, repeatedly move the fingertips towards the lip with short movements.

As if putting food in ones mouth.

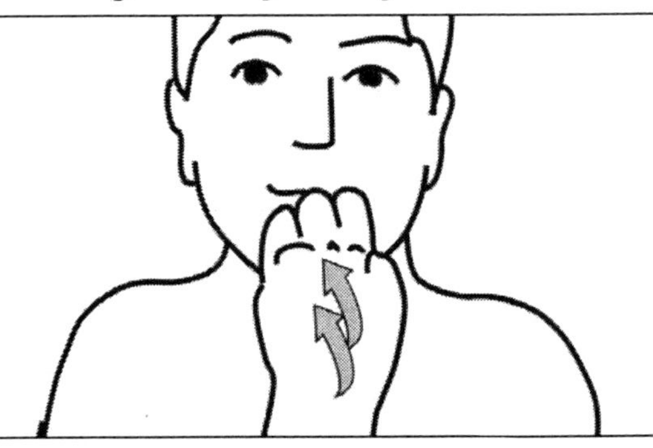

father - padre

Place the thumb of the dominant "5" hand on the forehead.

finish – fin, acabar

Hold the “5” hands in front of you, palms facing you, quickly twist hands to palms down.

[also: finished, completed, done, ended, over]

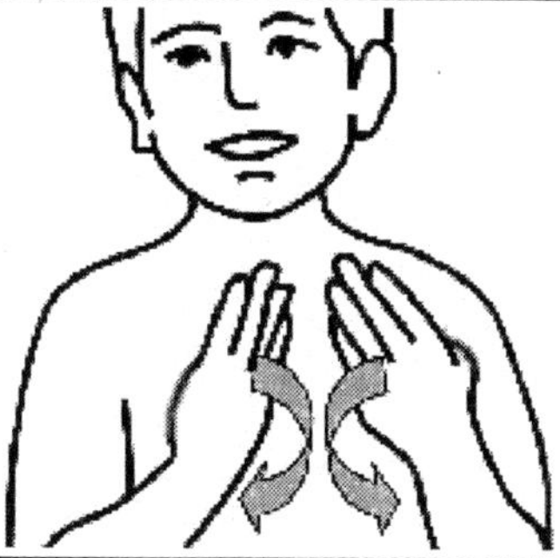

hear, oír, escuchar

Point the index finger towards the ear.

As if showing the ear to listen.

[also: ear]

milk - leche

Begin with the "C" hand in front of the body, tighten the hand to an "S" shape, repeatedly.

[As if milking a cow.]

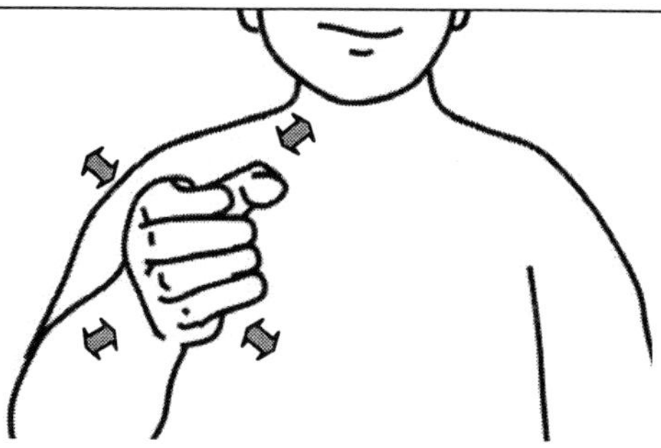

more - más

Bring the tips of both "flat O" hands together twice.

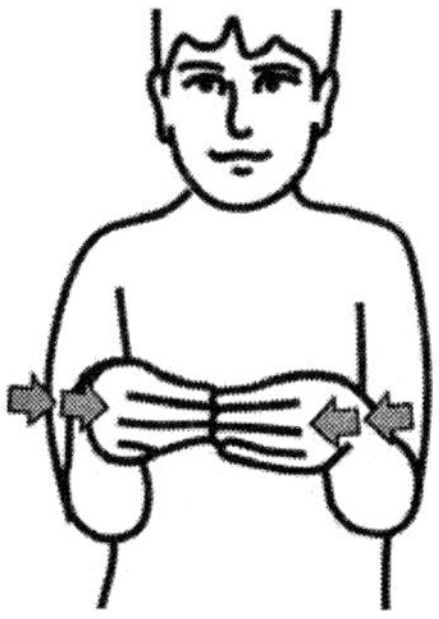

mother - madre

Place the thumb of the “5” hand on the chin.

up – hacia arriba Point up with the index finger of the dominant hand.	
water - agua Touch the mouth with the index finger of the "W" hand a few times.	

ACTIVITIES

- Read books, sign songs daily, include lullabies
- Introduce new vocabulary/signs in a meaningful context
- Speak directly to child – Wait – Give them time to respond
- Support "conversation" – Turn taking social/language skills
- Visual stimulation
- Body language games (This Little Piggy, Head and Shoulders)
- Environmental sounds (bring carrier while you do dishes, laundry, explain noises)
- Change child's position to give different perspective (sling, carrier, high chair, and floor)
- Give baby lots of opportunities for "tummy-time"
- Play peek-a-boo
- Encourage vocal play (vowel sounds "ooo" "aaah", consonant-vowel ba… da… Building to consonant-vowel-consonant: bababa … gagaga)
- Have "gooooo gooooo parties" or blow raspberries at each other…
- Introduce animals and their signs via puppets and stuffed animals

7 to 12 Months
DEVELOPMENTAL MILESTONES

- Imitates speech sounds – babbles
- Says “dada” and “mama”
- Combines syllables into word-like sounds
- Waves “bye-bye”
- Plays pat-a-cake
- Imitates others’ activities
- Produces word-like sounds
- Indicates wants with gestures
- Responds to name and understands “no”
- Begins to say additional word or two – other than “mama” and “dada”
- Understands and responds to simple instructions
- Sits without support

SIGNS

banana	please	book
bath	thank you	hurt
drink	shoes	head
help	ear ache	socks
hot	no touch	jump

banana - plátano

Move the closed fingertips of the dominant hand, down the extended reference index finger.

As if peeling your index finger.

bath -baño

For wash rub the "A" hands together palm to palm.

For bath rub the "A" hands on the chest near the shoulder.

[also: scrub, wash]

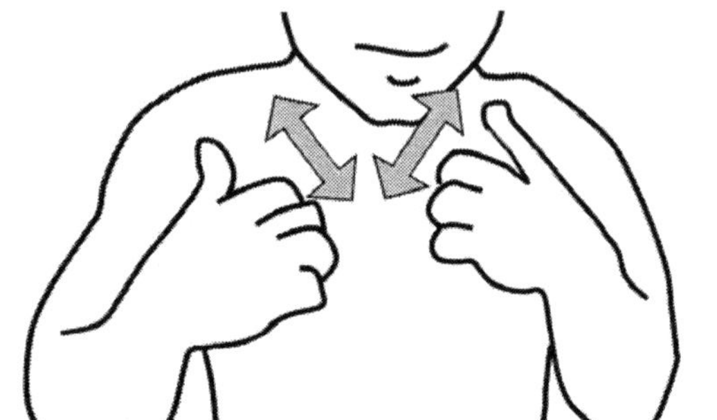

book - libro

Starting with both palms touching in front of the chest, fingers pointing forward, move the hands apart, keeping the little fingers together.

As if opening a book.

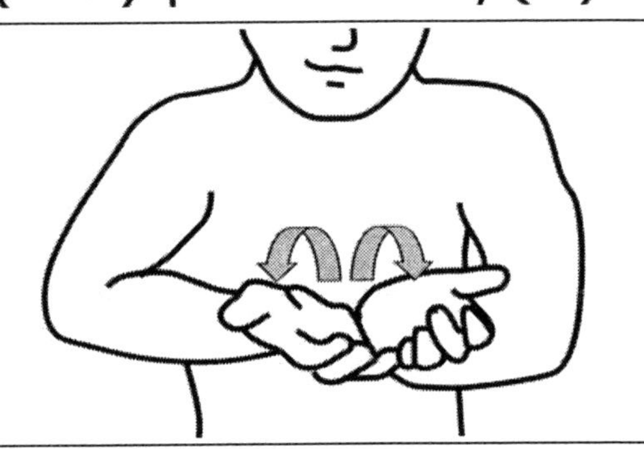

drink – bebida, tomar, beber

Use the "C" hand in front of the mouth and thumb touching bottom lip; then keeping the thumb in place, move fingers upward toward the nose.

As if taking a drink with the hands.

earache – dolor de oídos

Jab both index fingers toward each other several times in front of ear.

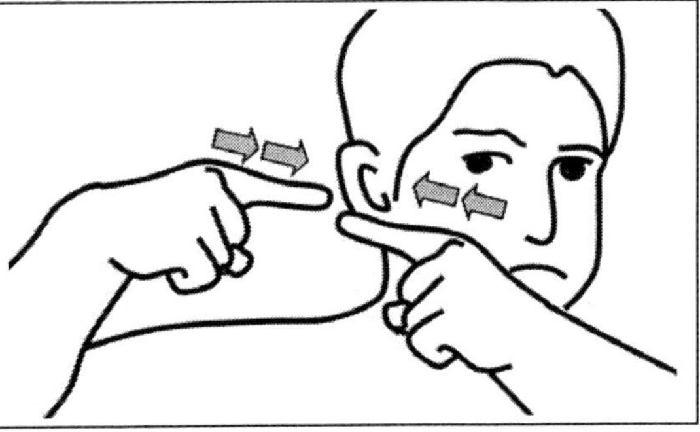

head - cabeza

Place the fingertips of the dominant bent hand against the same-sided temple and then move the dominant hand downward in an arc to the jaw.

help - ayuda

Place the dominant open hand under the reference "A" hand, thumb up, lift both hands together.

[also: aid, assist]

hot - caliente

Place the dominant "C" hand at the mouth, palm facing in; give the wrist a quick twist, so the palm faces out.

[also: heat]

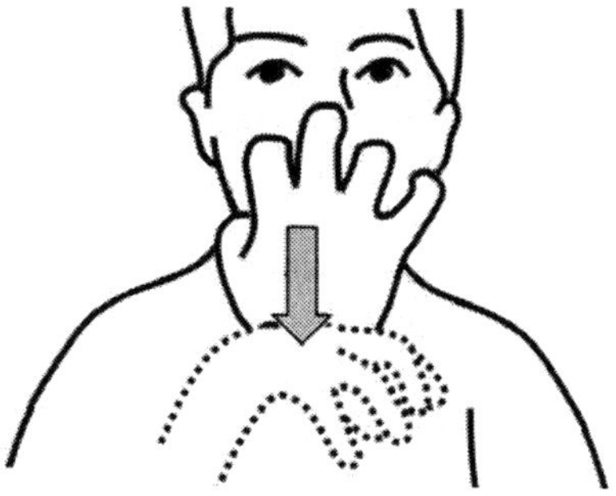

hurt - dolor

The index fingers are jabbed toward each other several times.

[also: pain, ache]

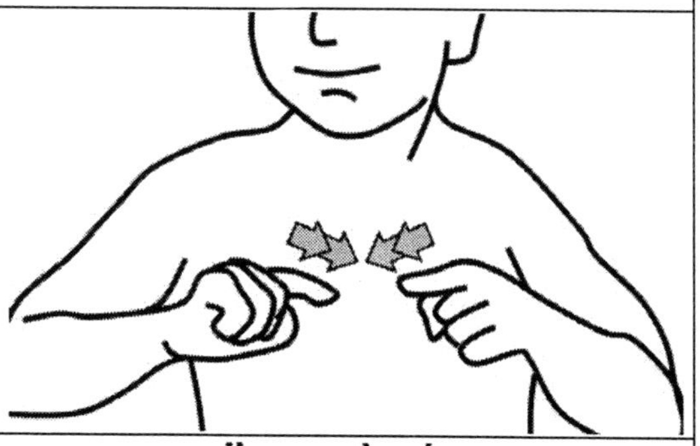

jump – saltar, brincar

Place the dominant "V" handshape in a standing position on the reference palm; lift the "V", bending the knuckles and return to a standing position.

touch – toque, tocar

Touch the back of the reference hand with the dominant middle finger, other fingers extended.

Senses – touch - tacto

no touch

- Shake your head no while making the touch sign.

please – por favor

Rub the chest with the open hand in a circular motion (palm facing yourself)

As if rubbing your heart.

[also: pleasure, enjoy, like]

shoes -zapatos

Strike the sides of the "S" hands together several times.

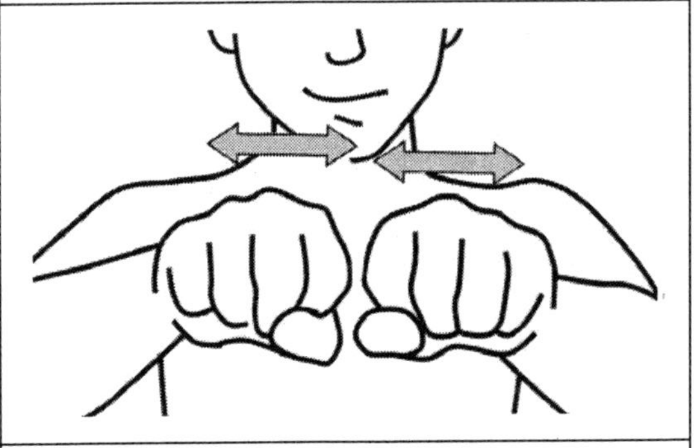

socks – calcetín

Place the index fingers side-by-side and rub them back and forth several times, tilting downwards.

As if two knitting needles are making socks.

[also: stockings, hose]

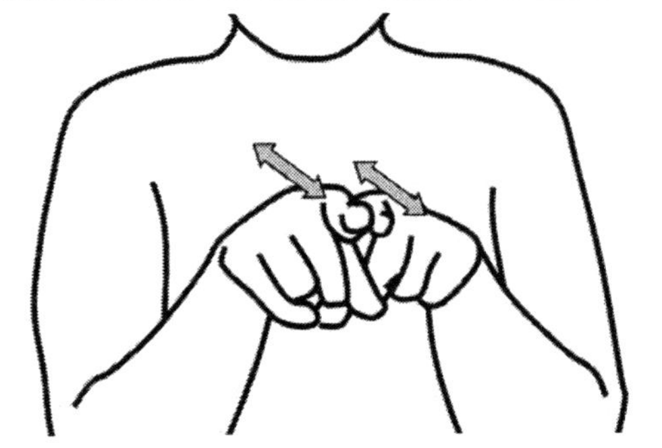

thank you - gracias

Touch lips with the fingertips of flat hand, then move the hand forward until the palm is facing up and towards the indicated person. Smile and nod head while doing this sign.

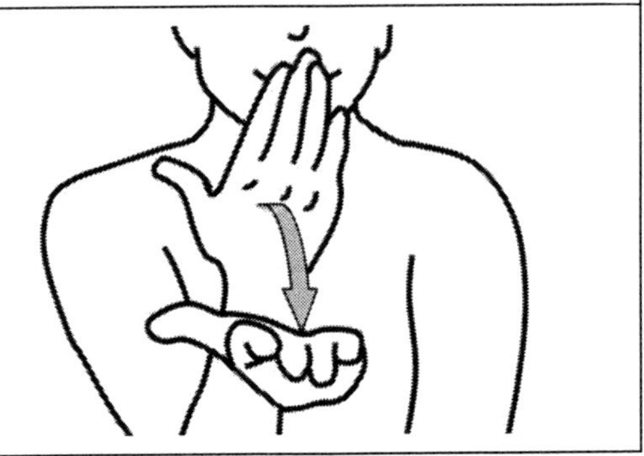

ACTIVITIES

- Books!! Books!!! – Build story time routines, especially at bedtime!
- Baby's own picture book – Make it with Grandma or Grandpa!
- Give back baby's words using adult language
- Naming walks around house/outside
- Bath time play
- Animal sounds – songs like Animals on the Farm and Old MacDonald
- Puppets are great fun for language play/games – Make your own from paper bags or socks – use non-toxic markers. Recycle the paper – wash the socks for more play!
- Body parts – Play exercise games touching baby's foot to hands – alternate right hand with left foot – Make reference to top of body vs. bottom of body; left side and right side; use position words such as "up" and "down"
- Mirror games
- All gone games
- Grab bag games

13 to 18 Months

DEVELOPMENTAL MILESTONES

- Uses two words skillfully – e.g., "hi", "bye"
- Imitates others
- Vocabulary increases, uses words more often
- Turns the pages of a book
- Enjoys pretend games
- Will "read" board books on his own
- Scribbles well
- Enjoys gazing at their reflection
- Plays "peek-a-boo"
- Points to one body part when asked
- Adopts "no" as their favorite word
- Responds to directions – "Sit down"
- Speaks more clearly
- Strings words together in phrases

SIGNS

moon	stop	airplane
hug	where	want
mine	yes	apple
no	fish	dog
toilet	cookie	bed

airplane – aeroplano, avión

Use the "Y" hand, with index finger extended and palm facing down. Make forward upward sweeping motion.

As if flying an airplane across the sky.

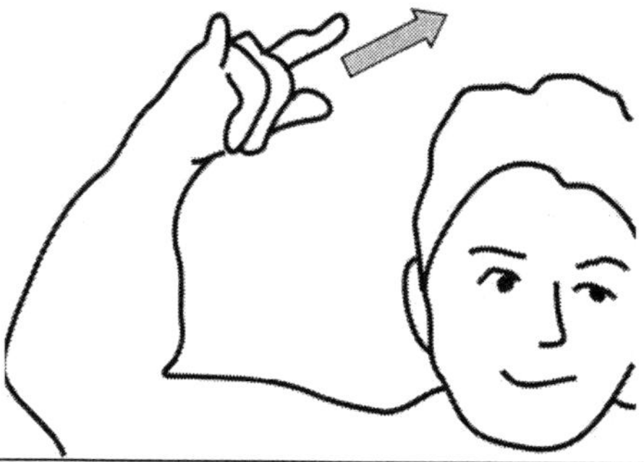

apple - manzana

With the knuckle of the bent index finger on the dominant cheek, twist downward.

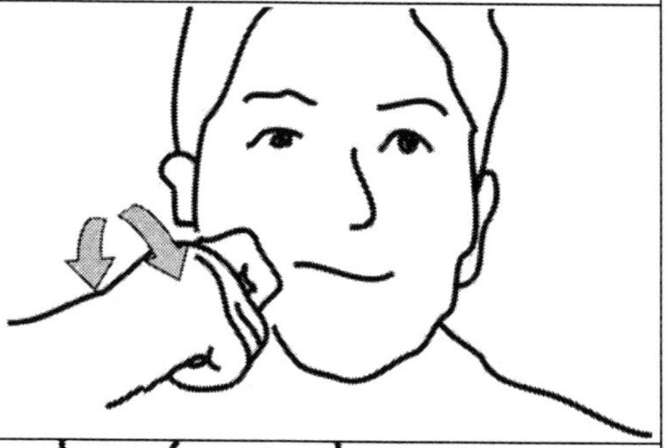

bed – cama, acostarse

Place the slightly curved dominant hand on the same-sided cheek and tilt the head to the side.

As if laying down your head on the hand.

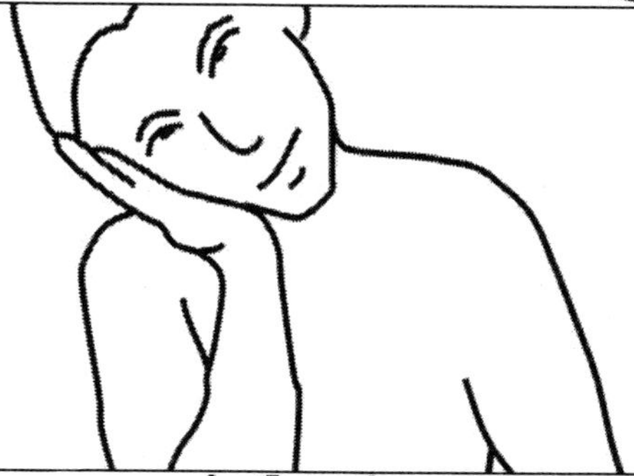

cookie - galleta

Touch the fingers of the dominant clawed "5" hand on the upturned reference palm and then twist the dominant hand and touch the reference palm again.

As if cutting cookies with a cookie cutter.

dog - perro

Snap the middle finger against the thumb. Can also add slapping the upper leg.

As if calling a dog.

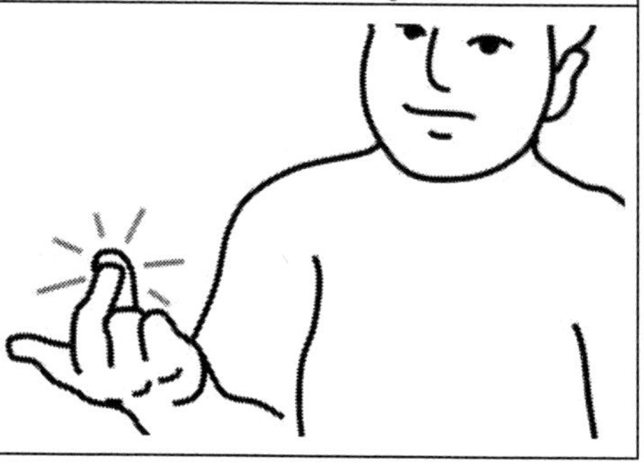

fish - pez

Begin with the dominant open hand palm facing the reference side and the reference extended index finger on the heel of the dominant hand. Swing the dominant hand back and forth with a double movement.

Like a fish swimming.

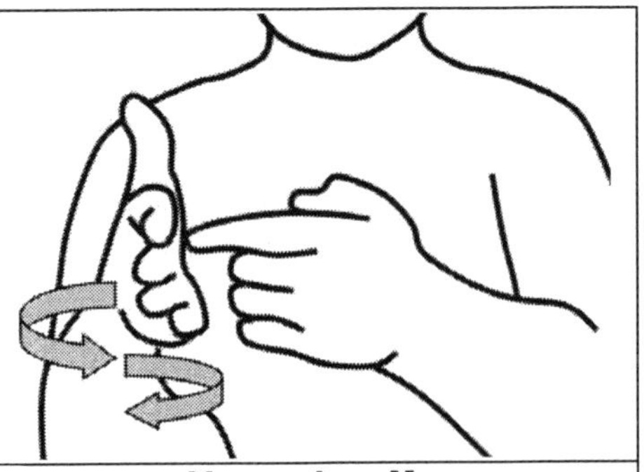

hug- abrazo, abrazar

The hands hold the upper arms as if hugging yourself.

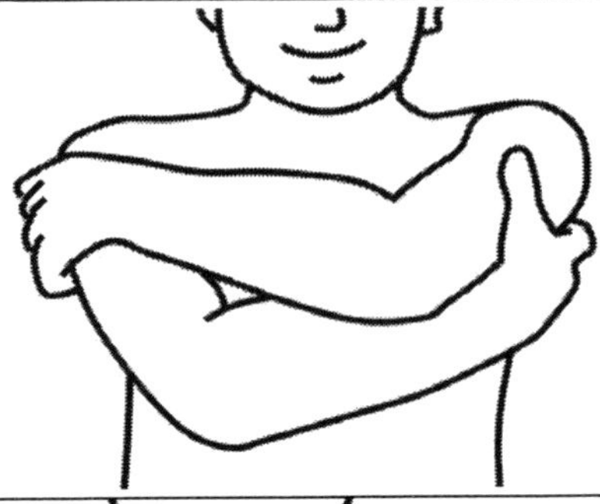

mine - mío

Place the dominant open hand on the chest.

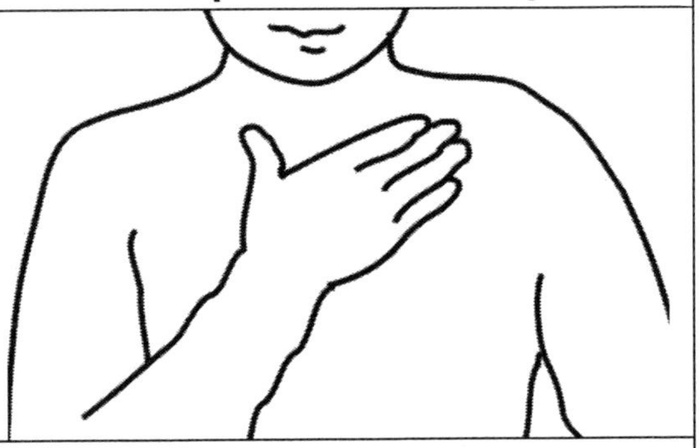

moon - luna

Tap the thumb of the modified "C" hand over the dominant eye, palm facing forward, with a double movement.

The symbol represents the crescent moon.

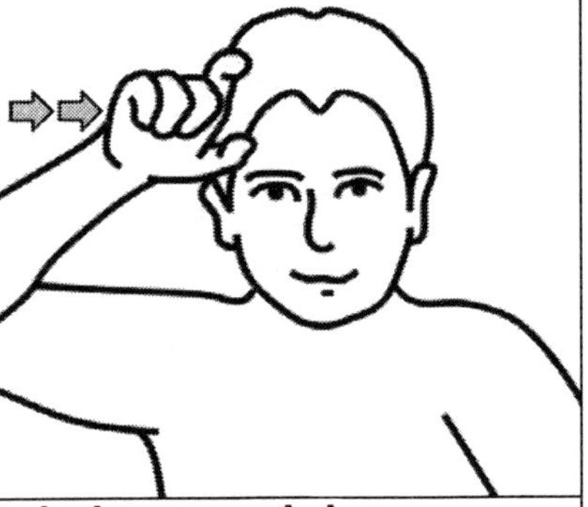

no - no

Bring the index, middle finger, and thumb together in one motion.

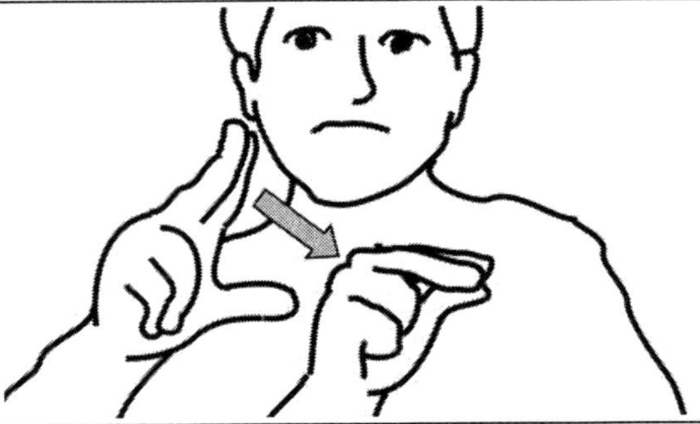

stop – parar, alto, detener, poner fin

Bring the little finger side of the dominant open hand abruptly down on the upturned reference palm.

As if chopping on something.

toilet – tocador, cuarto de baño, inodoro

Shake the dominant “T” hand from side to side in front of the body, palm facing forward.

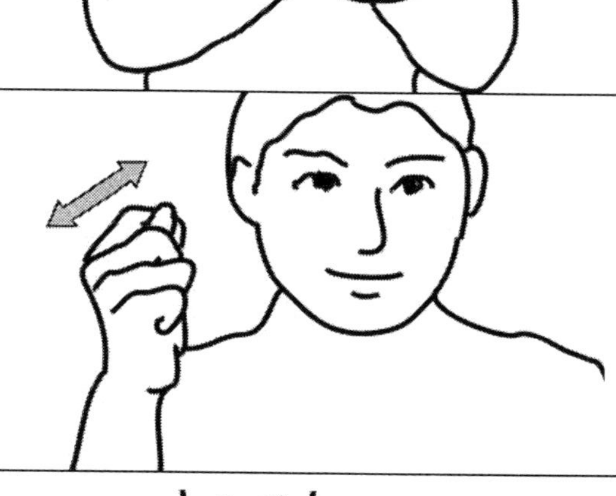

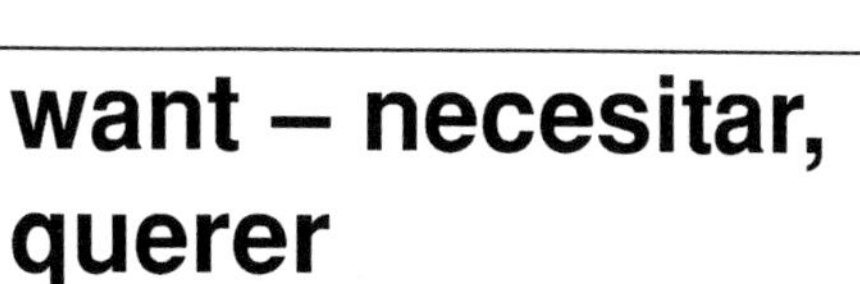

want – necesitar, querer

Place both “curved 5" hands in front of you, palms up, and draw them towards you.

As if gesturing to bring something to you.

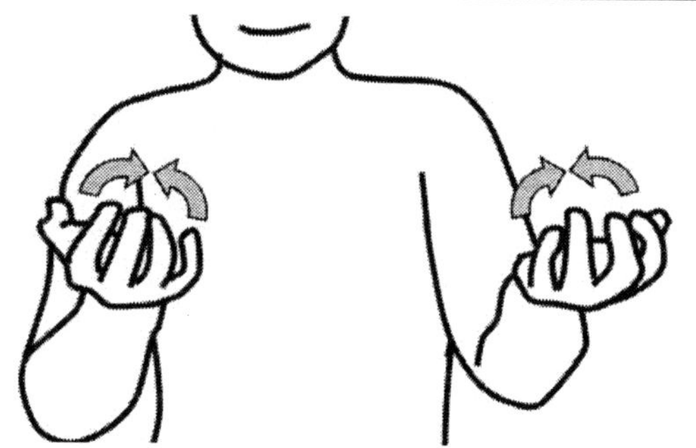

where - dónde

Hold up the dominant index finger and shake the hand back and forth quickly from reference to dominant.

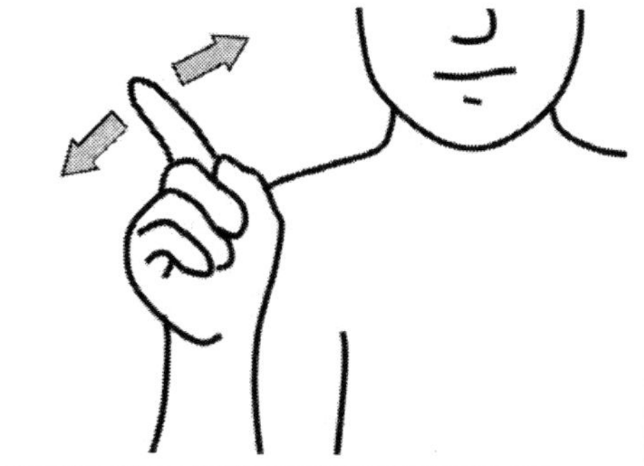

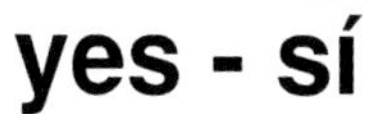

yes - sí

Shake the "S" hand up and down in front of you.

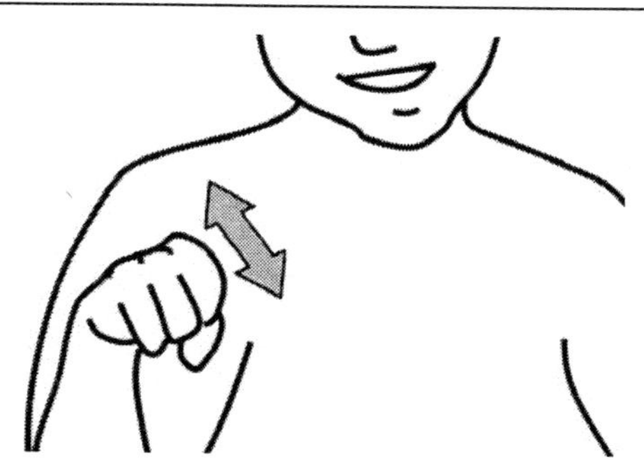

ACTIVITIES

- Ball Play – Rolling back and forth; throwing/bouncing (sponge and soft balls)
- Music Games – Finger play (Itsy Bitsy Spider)
- Books!!! – Reading to Child
- Animal "Talk" – Trips to zoo/farm – "Let's move/walk/sound like an elephant…monkey…kangaroo, etc."
- Pretend Play – Imitate Daily Living Activities
- Pull/push/ride toys
- Conversation games (jargon is child imitating adult intonation pattern)
- Blocks – Stacking toys; nesting and sorting toys
- Flash cards with animals and common objects
- Grab bag
- Coloring – Supervised
- Water color – Use plain water with paintbrush on sidewalk. Or, if you need to be inside – paint the Sunday comics (they'll feel like their painting and the comics are in color!)
- Shaving cream on tabletop or cookie sheet – great sensory activity – Careful to keep hands out of mouth and eyes!
- Finger paint with pudding – Use vanilla flavor and add food coloring to make a few choices.

19 to 24 Months

DEVELOPMENTAL MILESTONES

- Recognizes when something is stated incorrectly – e.g. someone calls a cat a dog
- Learns words at a rate of 10 or more a day
- Searches for hidden objects
- Follows two-step requests – "Get your toy and bring it here"
- Can name a simple picture in a book
- Can use 50 single words
- Half of speech is understandable
- Produces short sentences
- Capable of identifying several body parts
- Produces two or three word sentences
- Sings simple tunes
- Begins talking about self

SIGNS

happy	butterfly	wait
rain	friend	car
cat	bird	fish
cold	telephone	hard
soft	sad	rough
angry		

angry – colérico , enojado, enfadado

Place the clawed "5" hands against the waist and draw up against the sides of the body.

As if anger is boiling up out of person.

[also: wrath]

bird - pájaro

With the "G" hand at the mouth, palm forward, repeatedly open and close the index finger.

As if displaying a birds beak.

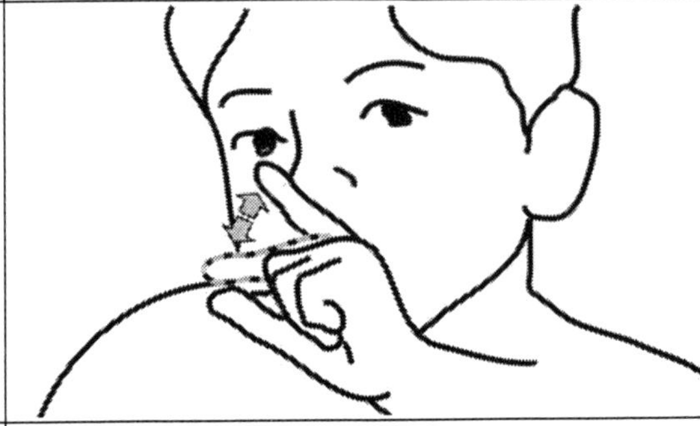

butterfly - mariposa

With the hands crossed at the wrist, palms toward the chest, and the thumbs of the open hands hooked together, flex and straighten several times.

As if demonstrating how a butterfly's wings flutter.

car – carro, coche, auto

Place the "S" hands in front of you, palms facing each other, and alternate clockwise then counter- clockwise as if driving a car.

As if steering a car.

[also: automobile, drive]

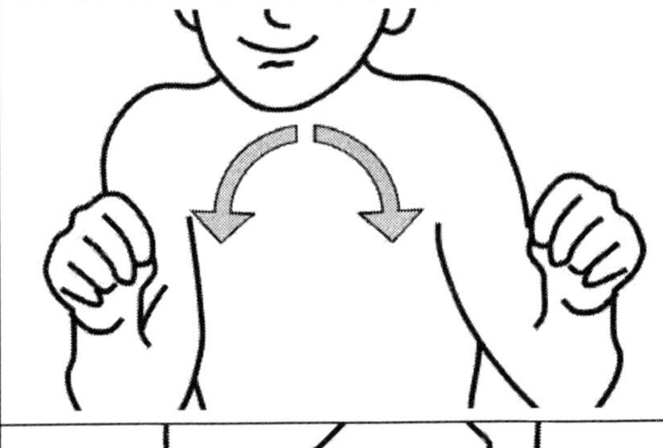

cat – gato(a)

The "F" hand touches the corner of the upper lip, brushing out and away from the face a couple of times.

As if you are stroking a cat's whiskers.

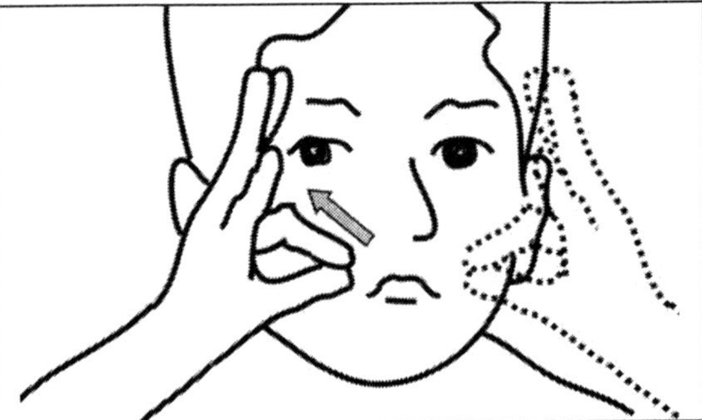

cold - frio

Shake both "S" hands, palms facing each other.

"Brr!"

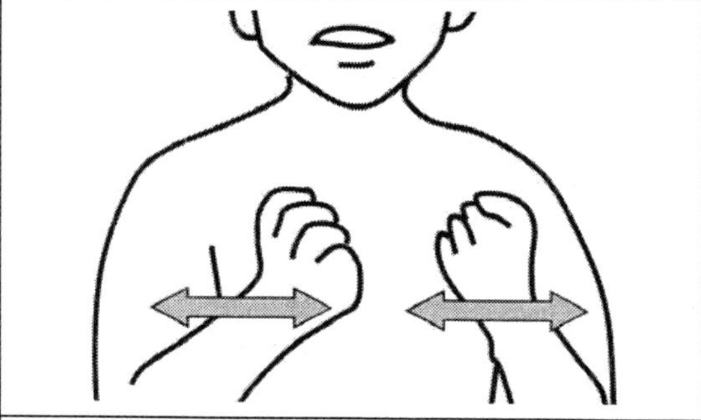

fish - pez

Begin with the dominant open hand palm facing the reference side and the reference extended index finger on the heel of the dominant hand. Swing the dominant hand back and forth with a double movement.

Like a fish swimming.

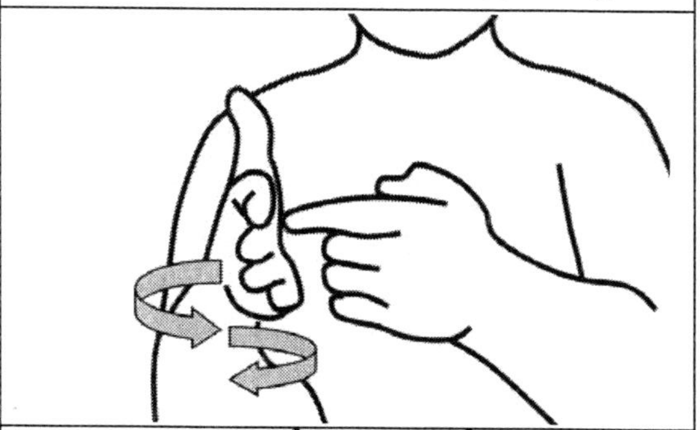

friend – amigo(a)

Interlock dominant "X" hand index finger down over upturned reference "X" hand index finger.

As if holding hands with someone.

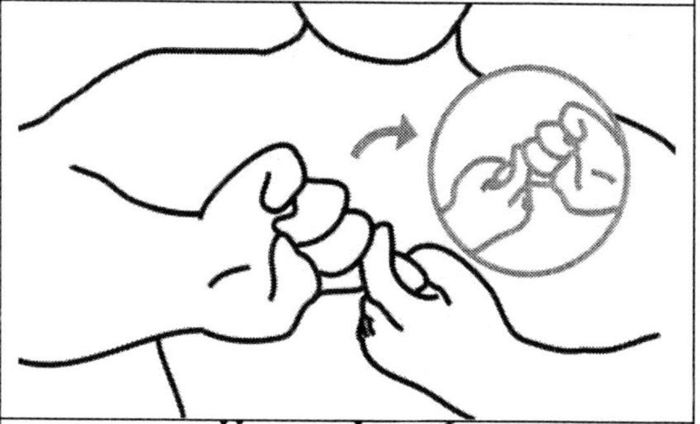

happy – alegre, feliz, contento

The open hands pat the chest several times with a slight upward motion.

As if heart is pounding with joy.

[also: glad, rejoice, joy]

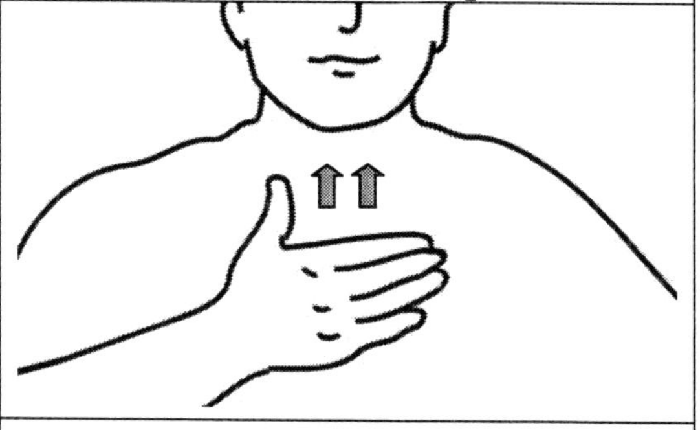

hard – duro, difícil

With both hands in the "bent V" handshape, tap the dominant hand on the reference hand. Palms facing in the opposite direction.

rain - lluvia

Let both curved "5" hands, palms facing down, drop down several times in short, quick motions.

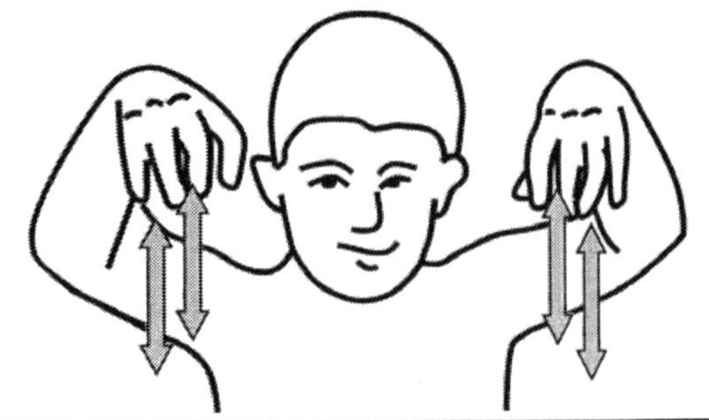

rough - tosco

Move the fingertips of the dominant curved 5 hand, palm facing down, from the heel to the fingertips of the upturned reference open hand.

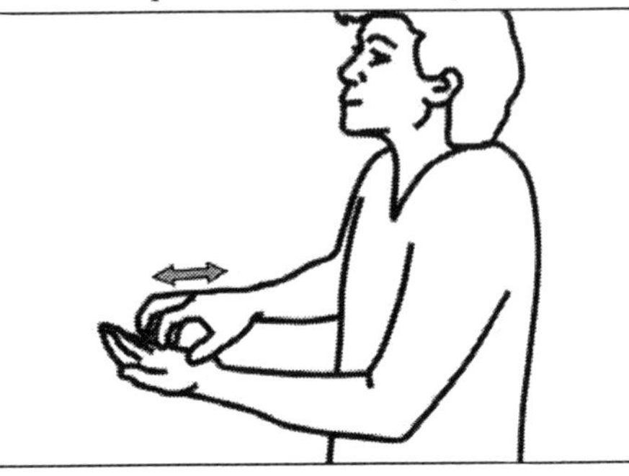

sad - triste

Hold both open hands in front of the face, fingers slightly apart and pointing up; then drop both hands a short distance and bend the head slightly.

[also: dejected, sorrowful, downcast]

soft – blando, ablandar, suave

Beginning with both "flat O" handshape in front of the shoulders, bring the hands down with a double movement while rubbing the fingers against the thumbs each time.

As if the fingers are feeling soft.

telephone - teléfono

Place the thumb of the "Y" hand on the ear and the little finger at the mouth.

As if talking on the phone.

[also: call]

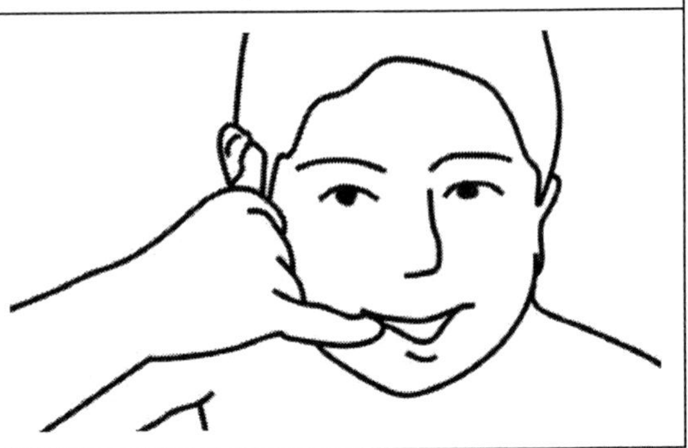

wait – espera, esperar

Beginning with both curved "5" hands in front of the body, reference palm up in front of the dominant palm up, wiggle the fingers.

As if asking for something.

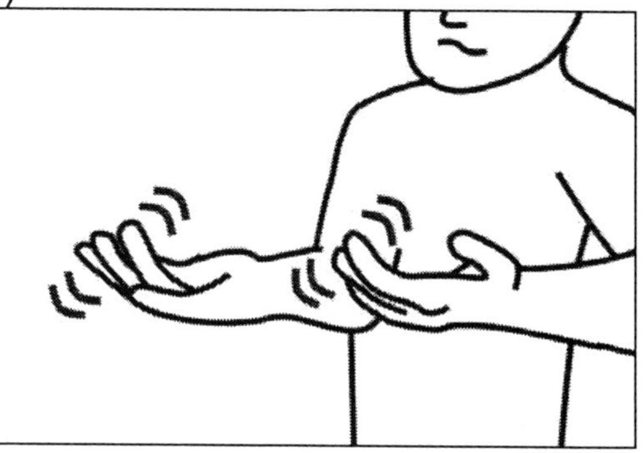

ACTIVITIES

- Happy/sad emotion face games
- Hide objects behind your back – Which hand? – "shell games"
- Books!!! Books!!! Use puppets to retell stories – extend and make up your own stories!
- Dress up and dramatic play games
- Cars – Trains – Provide lots of containers for them to use and blocks to make roads.
- Hide-and-seek – Introduce counting – very simple rules.
- Texture boxes – Cut scraps from old clothing with interesting and different materials.
- Sensory Play – Sand/water/dough/pudding, etc.
- Water Play – Use dolls in bathtub to name body parts – bath, brush teeth and hair – build social and self-help skills.
- Painting/Coloring activities – support play – support language and conversation – describe what your child is doing and what you are doing – Play with your child. Get on the floor with them!

25 to 30 Months

DEVELOPMENTAL MILESTONES

- Names several body parts
- Speaks clearly most to all of the time
- Understands emotional expressions
- Answers "wh" questions
- Uses up to 200 words
- Asks simple questions
- Comprehends up to 500 words
- Listens to a 5-10 minute story

SIGNS

cow	good	monkey	stop
down	grandmother	snake	throw
fish	hide	snow	toilet
frog	horse	sorry	work

cow - vaca With the thumbs of the "Y" hands at the temples, bend the wrists forward a few times. Shows a cow's horns. As if showing a bull's horns.	
down - abajo Point down with the index finger.	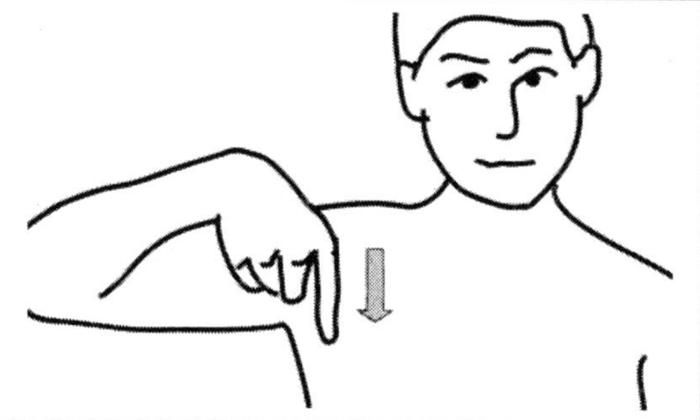
frog - rana Begin with "S" hand under the chin, flick the index and middle fingers outward. As if to indicate the filling of air into the frog's throat.	
good – bueno(a), bien Starting with fingertips of the open hand on the lips, move the hand down to touch the open palm. As if something tasted good and you want more.	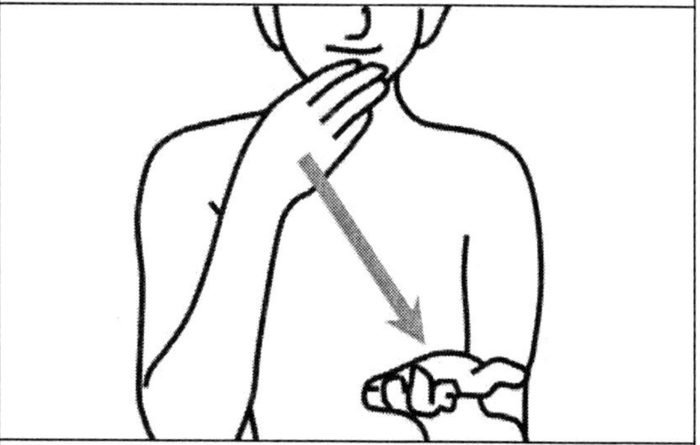
grandmother - abuela Sign "mother". Place the thumb of the "5" hand on the chin, then bounce forward once. Indicates one generation away from mother.	

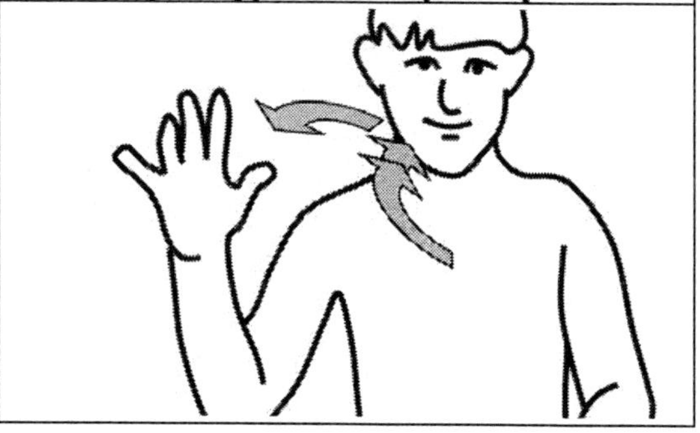

hide – esconder, esconderse, ocultar Move the thumb of the dominant "A" hand under the reference curved hand, palm facing down. Gesture putting something under the other hand as if to hide it.	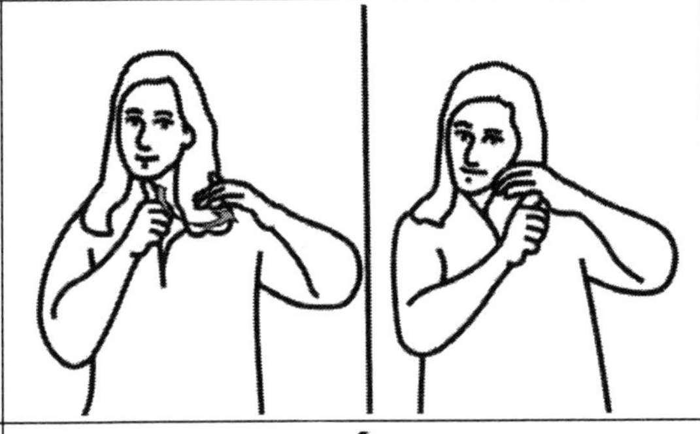
horse - caballo With the "U" hand beside the temple, bend and unbend the index and middle fingers. Indicates a horse's ears.	
monkey - mono Scratch the ribs on both sides of the body with the curved "5" hands. As if scratching characteristics of monkeys.	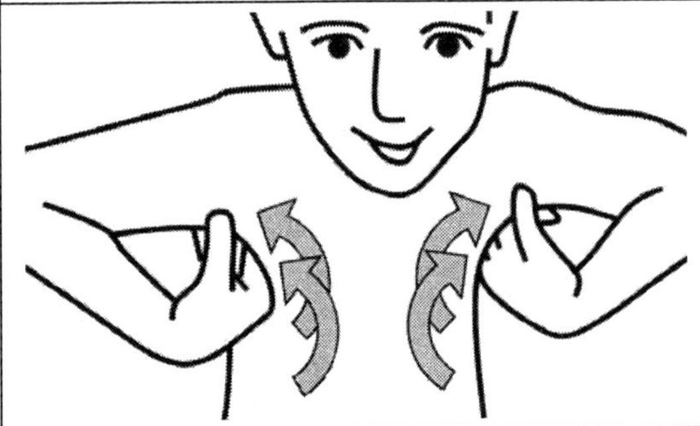
snake – culebra, serpiente Sharply move the "bent V" handshape in a spiral movement. Indicates a snake preparing to strike with its fangs.	
snow - nieve Let both "5" hands, palm down, drop down while gently wiggling the fingers. As if snowflakes pointing downward.	

sorry – lo siento, lo lamento

Rub the palm side of the dominant "S" hand in a large circle on the chest with a repeated movement.

Indicates rubbing the heart in sorrow.

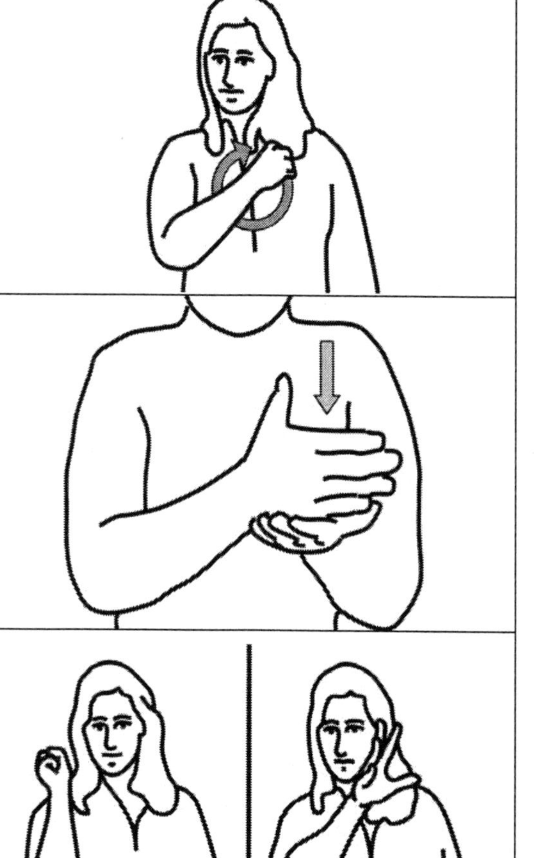

stop – alto, parar, detener, poner fin

Bring the little finger side of the dominant open hand abruptly down on the upturned reference palm.

As if chopping on something.

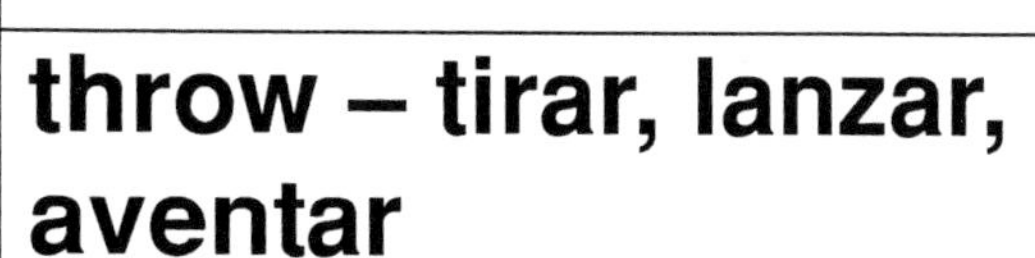

throw – tirar, lanzar, aventar

Beginning with the dominant "S" hand in front of the dominant shoulder, move the hand forward and downward while opening into a 5 hand.

As if throwing something.

walk – paseo, andar, caminar

Open hands, palms down, are moved in a forward-downward motion alternately

As if walking with the hands.

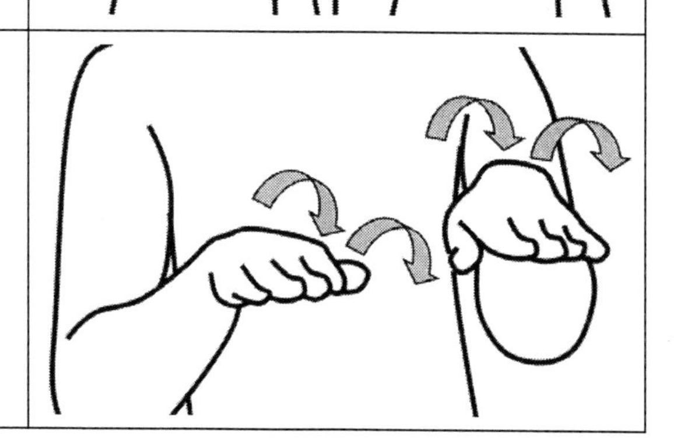

ACTIVITIES

- Sorting, matching, and counting games -- Use large craft buttons, blocks, etc.)
- In/on, over/under games – Hide and seek with objects.
- Books!!! Books!!!! Make your own books about family trips – daily routines – grocery shopping – going to the park, etc.
- Eye-hand coordination activities – Support fine and gross motor skills. Bean bag toss at a target; drop clothespins in a plastic bottle. Help your child to get them out – it's harder than it looks!
- "Once upon a Story…." – Together you and your child make up stories "on-the-spot" by taking turns adding 1-2 sentences each – building upon each other's pieces. Tape record the stories as you both get better and replay them later. Send them to relatives for presents!
- Make a tape w/ different sounds around the house
- "Simon Says" games – These are very fun when you're trying to get some chores done around the house – or cleaning out old toys.
- Make your own video with your child telling story, signing song, and then let them watch it. Also, makes a great gift for family and friends.

31 to 36 Months

DEVELOPMENTAL MILESTONES

- Names six or more body parts
- Names one color
- Carries on conversations of two to three sentences
- Describes how two objects are used
- Uses four to five words in a sentence
- Uses prepositions – on, in, over
- Follows a two or three part command
- Uses up to 500 words
- Comprehends up to 900 words
- Listens to 10 minute story
- Understands simple comparisons – big/little
- Repeats common rhymes

SIGNS

bear	coat	paper	square
bee	circle	pink	turtle
black	colors	purple	warm
blue	dance	rabbit	white
boy	flower	red	yellow
brother	girl	sister	
brown	orange	sit	

bear – oso, osa

Scratch the upper chest near the shoulders repeatedly with both "5" hands crossed in front of chest at the wrists.

As if giving a bear hug.

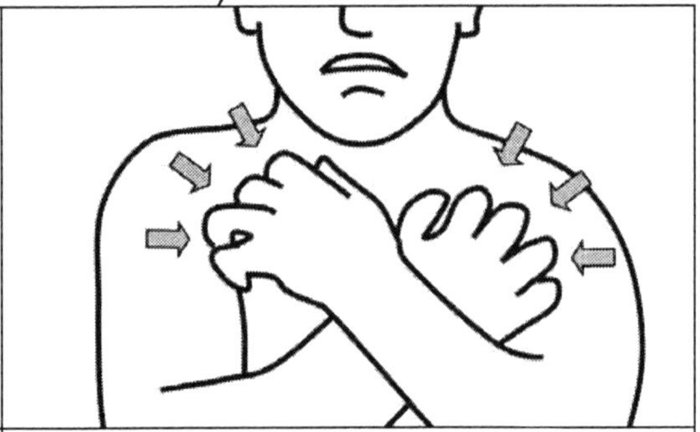

bee - abeja

Press the "F" hand against the dominant cheek. Then brush the index-finger side of the dominant "B" hand against the cheek.

Indicating the biting action of an insect then a natural gesture of brushing it away.

black - negro

Beginning with the center of the forehead, draw the index finger across the eyebrow.

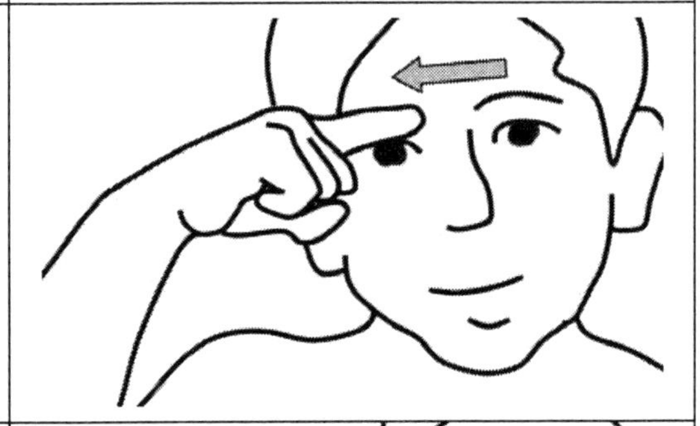

blue - azul

Shake the dominant "B" hand in front of the chest.

boy – niño, chico, muchacho

Beginning with the index-finger side of the dominant "C" hand near the dominant side of the forehead, close the fingers to the thumb with a repeated movement.

As if grasping the visor of a baseball cap.

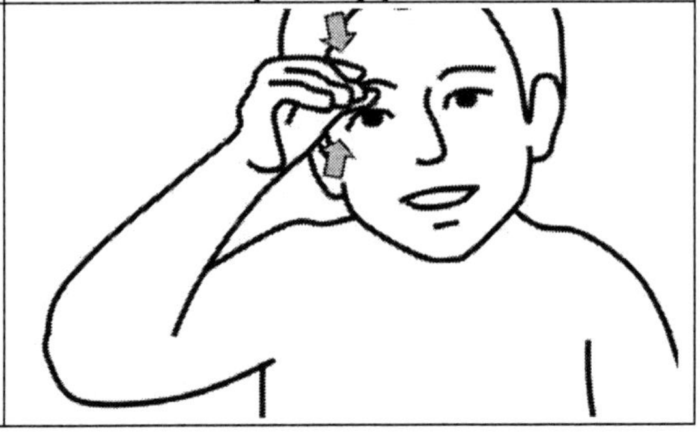

brother - hermano

Sign "BOY" and "SAME".
First move with the index-finger side of the dominant "C" hand near the dominant side of the forehead, close the fingers to the thumb with a repeated movement. Then place both index fingers side by side, pointing to the front.

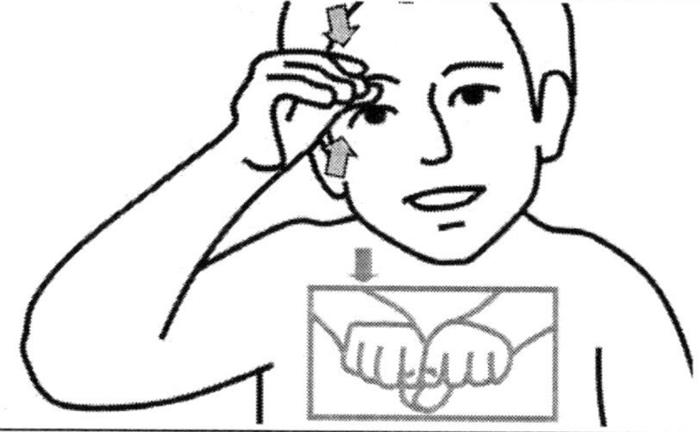

brown – marrón, color café

Move the index-finger side of the "B" hand down the dominant cheek.

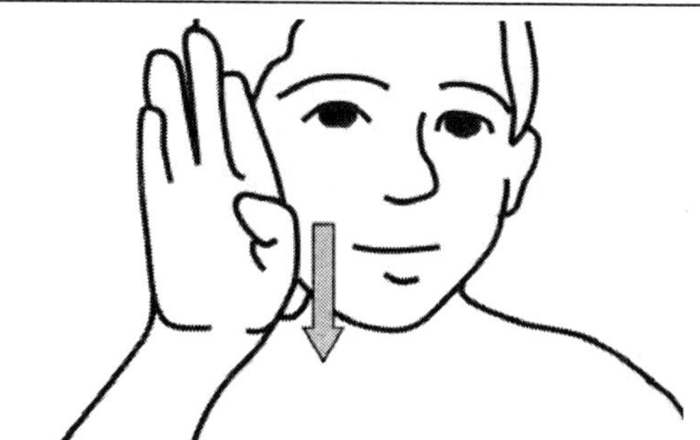

circle - círculo

Beginning with the "1" hand in front of the top of the chest, palm facing out, move the hand in a circular motion all the way back to point at which you began.

As if drawing a circle.

coat - abrigo

Bring the thumbs of both A hands from near each shoulder, palms facing in, downward and toward each other, ending near the waist.

Indicates a coat's lapels.

colors – colores, color

Place the "5" hand in front of the mouth and wiggle the fingers as the hand moves away slightly.

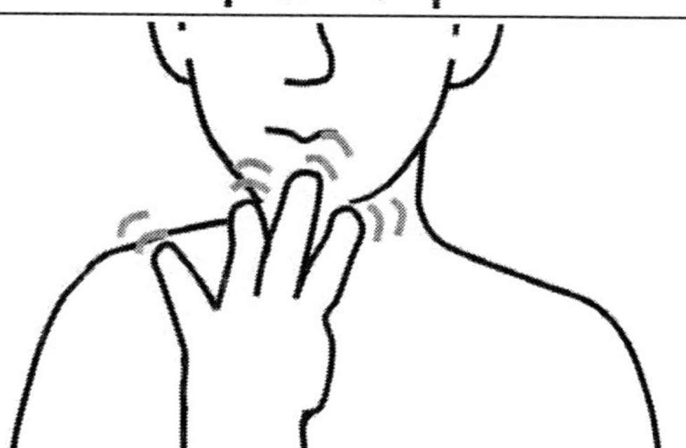

dance - baile Place the "V" in the standing position on the reference palm and swing the "V" back and forth. As if dancing with the fingers.	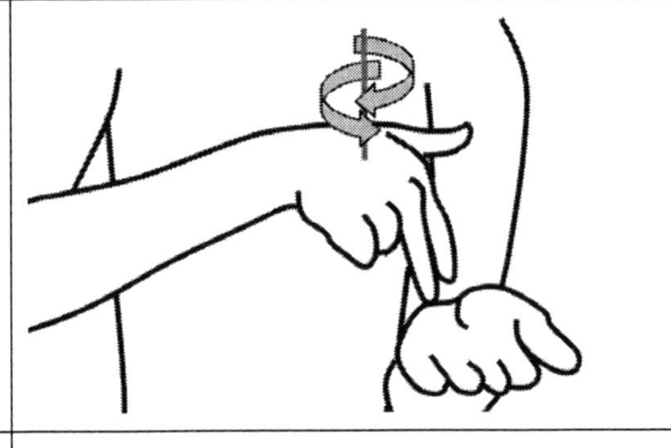
flower - flor First place the tips of the "flat O" hand first under one nostril, then under the other. As if smelling a flower.	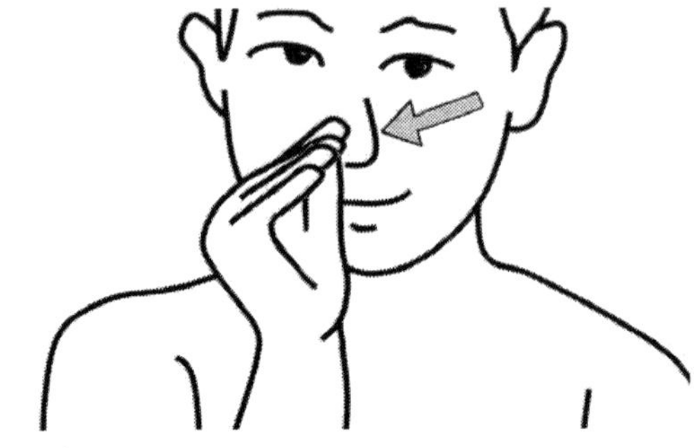
girl – niña, chica, muchacha Move the thumb of the dominant A hand, downward on the dominant cheek to the dominant side of the chin.	

orange – naranja Squeeze the "S" hand once or twice at the chin. Sign for the color the fruit. [Same sign for color or fruit] **orange – anaranjado** Squeeze the "S" hand once or twice at the chin. Sign for the color orange.	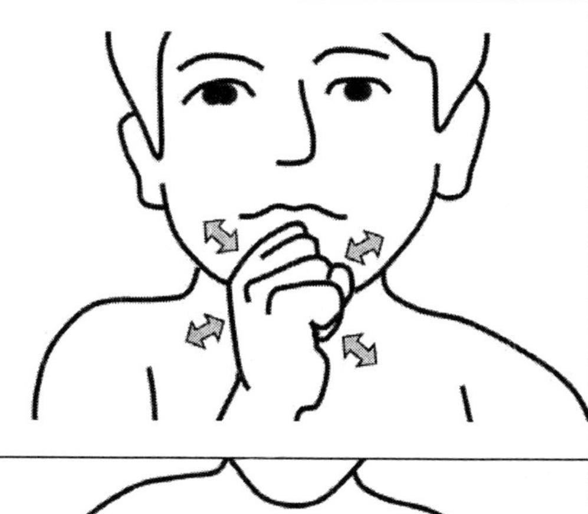
paper – papel Sweep the heel of the dominant "5" hand, palm down, back against the heel of the upturned reference "5" hand with an upward motion, in a double movement.	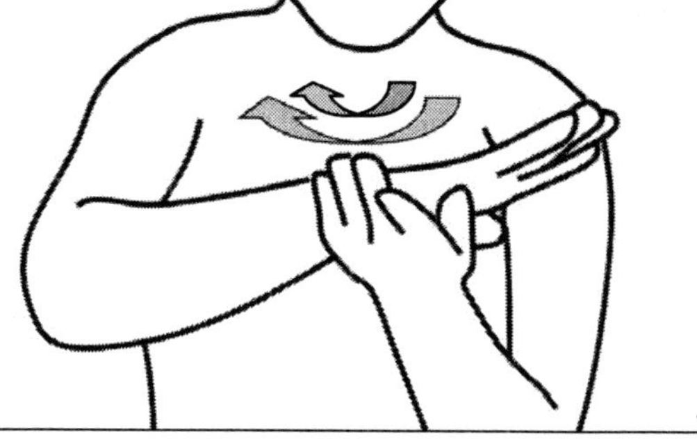

pink – rosa

Brush the middle finger of the dominant "P" hand, palm facing in, downward across the lips with a short repeated movement.

purple – púrpura, morado

Gently shake the fingers of the "P" handshape.

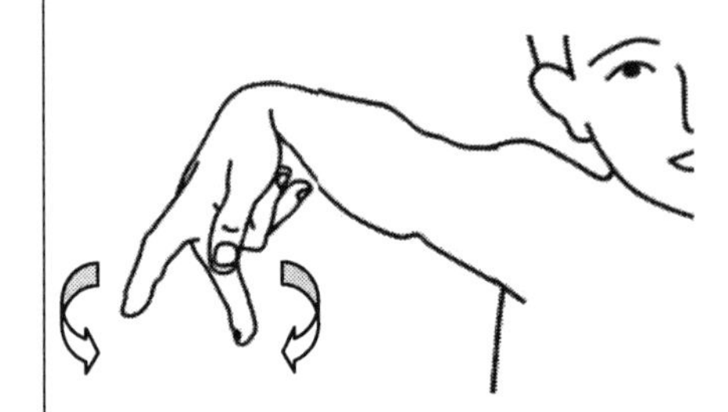

rabbit – conejo

With the "U" hands crossed above the wrists, palms facing in and thumbs extended, bend the fingers of both hands forward and back towards the chest with a double movement.

Indicates the rabbit's ears.

red - rojo

Move the inside tip of the dominant index finger down across the lips. Also, made with an "R" handshape.

sit - sentarse

Place the fingers of the "H" hand on top of the reference "H" hand, palms facing down, as if sitting on a bench.

As if two legs are dangling from a bench.

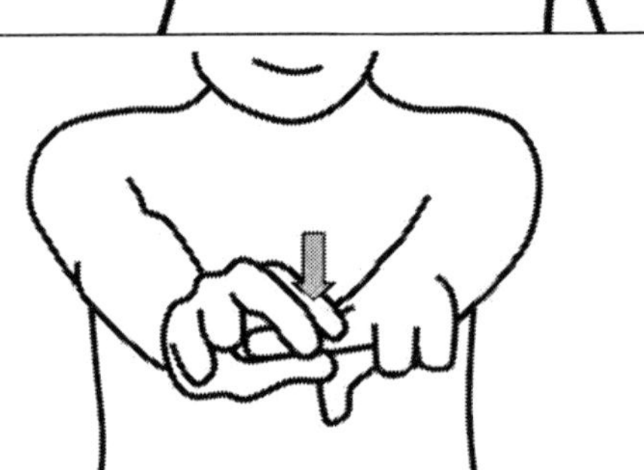

sister - hermana

Sign "GIRL", then "SAME".
First move the thumb of the dominant "A" hand, palm facing reference, downward on the dominant cheek to the dominant side of the chin. Then place both index fingers side by side, pointing to the front.

square – cuadro, cuadrado

With the dominant index finger, in front of the dominant shoulder, bring the dominant hand down, then to your reference, then up in front of your reference shoulder, then back across your body to where you began.

turtle - tortuga

Cup the reference palm over the dominant "A" hand and wiggle the dominant thumb with a repeated movement.

As if the turtle's head is coming out of its shell.

yellow - amarillo

Gently shake the "Y" handshape at chest level.

warm – calído

Beginning with the fingers of the dominant "E" hand near the mouth, palm facing in, move the hand forward in a small arc while opening the fingers into a C hand.

Indicates the warm air coming from the mouth.

white - blanco

Place fingertips of the "5" hand on the chest and move the hand forward into the flattened "O" hand.

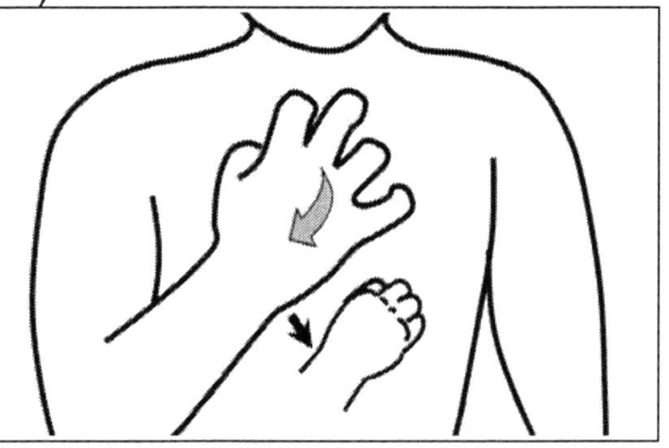

ACTIVITIES

- Tricycle – "big wheel" riding and peddle toy play
- Toilet Mastery – stories, introduce "potty language" and steps for using the toilet, e.g., pulling down pants, sitting, wiping, washing hands, etc.
- Activities that build on location words: in, on, under, top.
- Use comparison words: big/little, rough/smooth.
- Bean Bag Toss
- Felt Board Sequencing Activities
- Rhyming Stories/Poems – Mother Goose stories
- Color matching and sorting activities
- Connective Blocks – Building patterns with blocks
- Puzzles – Floor and table top – easy interlocking
- Shape sorters
- Coloring – Cutting and pasting – Arts 'n Crafts
- Simply cooking activities – great for language development and social/self help skills building.

37 to 42 Months

DEVELOPMENTAL MILESTONES

- Engages in longer dialogue
- Requests permission – "May I?"
- Corrects others when they misspeak
- Clarifies own conversation when misunderstood
- Uses up to 800 words
- Answers simple "how" questions
- Uses compound sentences with "and"
- Comprehends 1,200 words
- Emerging understanding of location – "in front of", "behind"
- Recognizes simple comparisons – hard/soft, rough/smooth
- Recognizes the names of simple shapes – circle, square

SIGNS

book	little	popcorn	Teacher
doctor	nurse	potato	Teacher's Aide
Firefighter	over	scared	tickle
game	out	scissors	tired
glue	play	spider	under
ice cream	police	spoon	worm
lion			

book - libro

Starting with both palms touching in front of the chest, fingers pointing forward, move the hands apart, keeping the little fingers together.

As if opening a book.

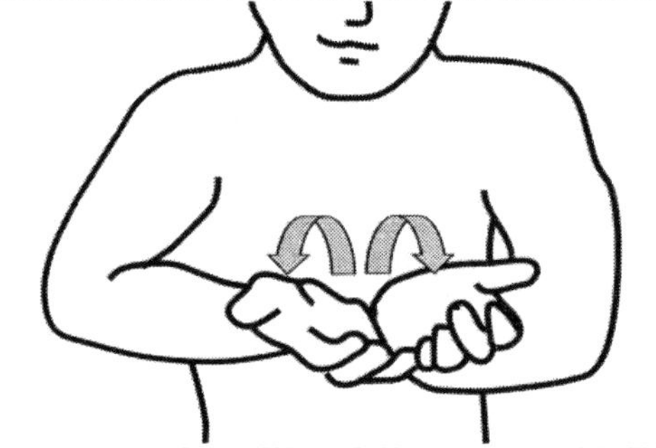

doctor – doctor(ora), médico

Tap the reference wrist, palm facing up, with the dominant “D” hand with a double movement.

As if taking your pulse.

firefighter - bombero

Bring the back of the dominant “B” hand, fingers pointing up and palm facing forward, against the center of the forehead.

Represents the raised front of the firefighter’s helmet.

game – juego, jugar

Bring the “A” hands towards each other, palms toward the body, in a slightly upward motion.

As if two people are facing each other in competition.

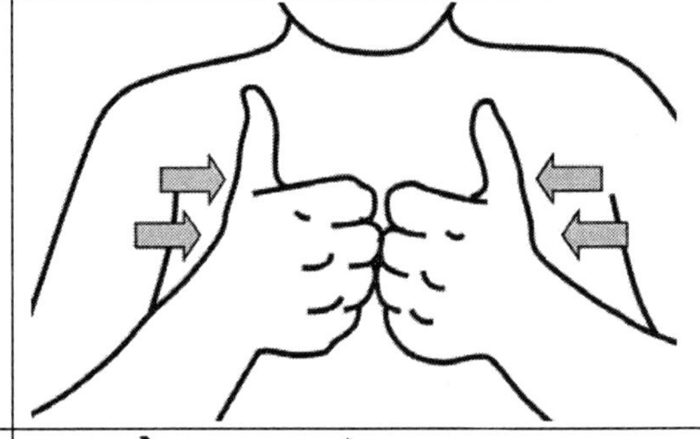

glue – cola de pegar, pega

Move the fingertips of the dominant "G" hand, palm and fingers facing down in a circular movement over the upturned reference open hand.

You can fingerspell G-L-U-E.

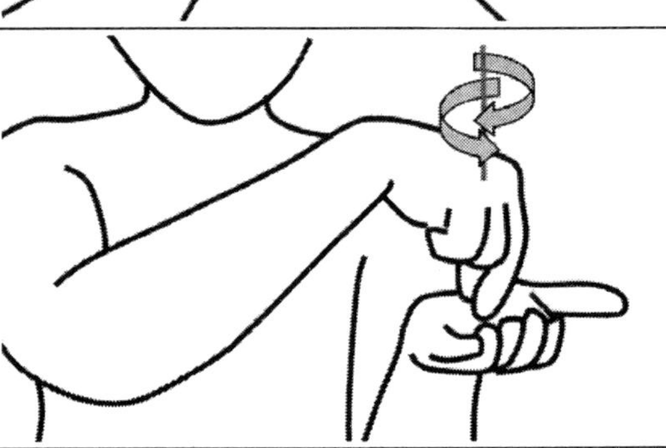

ice cream - helado

Bring the index-finger side of the dominant “S” hand, back in an arc towards the mouth with a double movement.

Indicates eating an ice cream cone.

lion - león

Beginning with the fingers of the dominant curved “5” hand pointing down over the forehead, move the hand back over the top of the head.

Indicates the lions mane.

little – pequeño, poco

Bring your hands close together as if to clap, stopping about 1” from touching.

Indicates size.

nurse - enfermera

Tap the extended fingers of the dominant N hand with a double movement on the wrist of the reference open hand held in front of the body, palm facing up.

As if checking your pulse.

out – fuera

The dominant "open 5" hand, facing the body and pointing down, becomes a “flat O" hand as it moves up through the reference "C" which then becomes an "O".

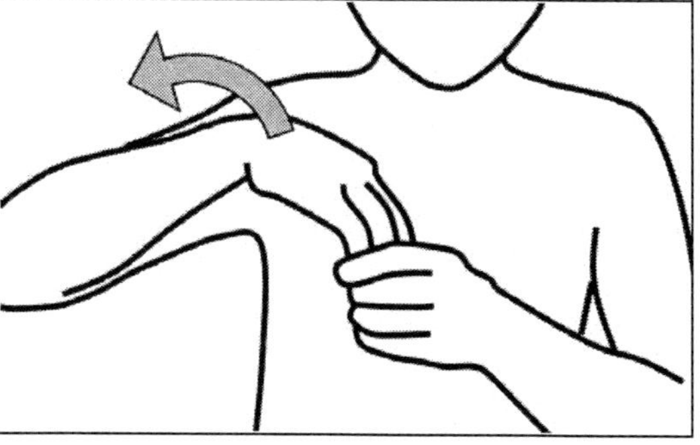

over – encima de, sobre, arriba de

With the fingertips of both bent hands touching in front of the chest, move the dominant hand up in a short arc.

play – juego, jugar

Place the "Y" hands in front of you and shake them in and out from the wrist a few times.

Indicates play as in recreation.

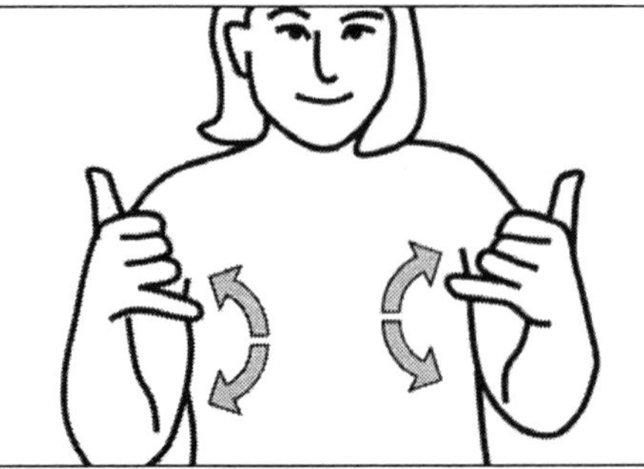

Police Officer - policía

Tap the thumb side of the dominant modified "C" hand, against the reference side of the chest with a double movement.

Indicates the badge.

popcorn – palomitas de maíz

Beginning with both "S" hands in front of each side of the body, alternatively move each hand upward while flicking out each index finger with a repeated movement.

Indicates the location of the police badge.

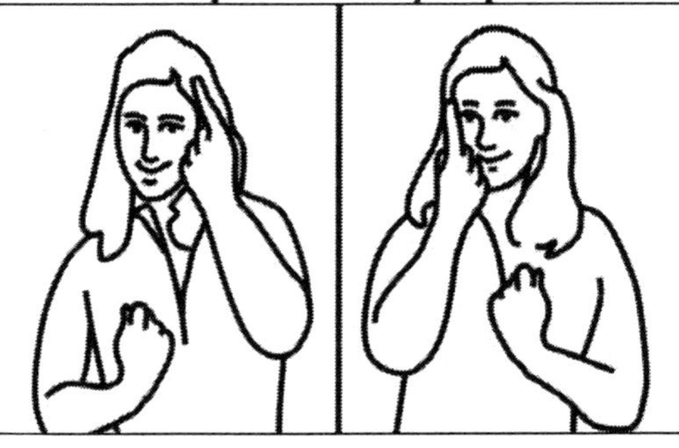

potato – papas, patata

Tap the fingertips of the dominant bent "V" hand, with a double movement on the back of the reference open hand.

Indicates putting fork tines into a baked potato to see if it is done.

scared – tener miedo, alarmar

Begin with both "A" hands in front of each side of the chest, spread the fingers open with a quick movement changing into "5" hands, palms facing in and fingers pointing toward each other.

[also: scared, frightened, terrify]

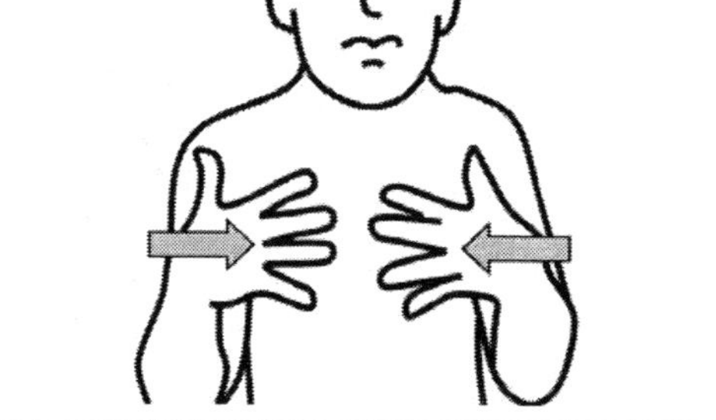

scissors - tijera

With the "H" hand turned, palm facing self, open and close fingers repeatedly.

As if your hand was a pair of scissors.

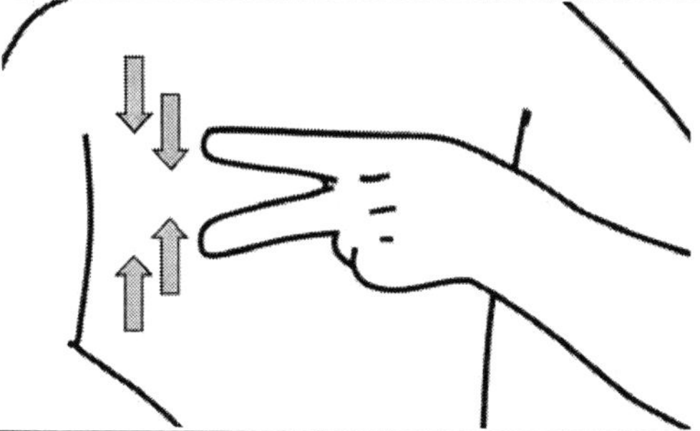

spoon - cuchara

Wipe the backs of the fingers of the dominant "U" hand, palm facing up and thumb extended, across the upturned palm of the reference opened hand from the fingers to the heel.

Indicates a spoon scooping up food.

spider - araña

With the hands crossed at the wrists, palms down, wriggle the fingers of both "claw" hands. Show the spider's legs crawling.

Indicates the leg movement of a spider.

Teacher, teach – maetra(o), enseñar

Move both "flattened O" hands, forward with a small double movement in front of each side of the head. Then with both open hands facing each other in front of the chest move them down to in front of the waist.

Sign "teach + "agent"

The hands seem to take information from the head and direct it to another person.

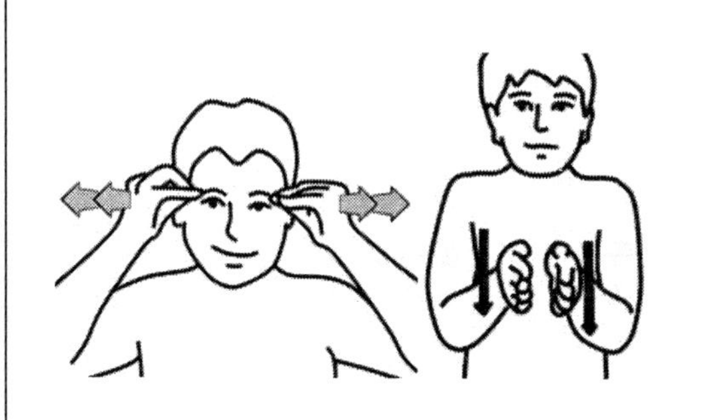

Teacher's Aide – maestro(a) asistente First move both flattened "O" hands, palms facing each other, forward with a small double movement in front of each side of the head. [The hands seem to take information from the head and direct it from another person.] Then use the thumb of the dominant "A" hand under the little-finger side of the reference "A" hand to push the reference hand upward in front of the chest. [Hands show a boost being given.]	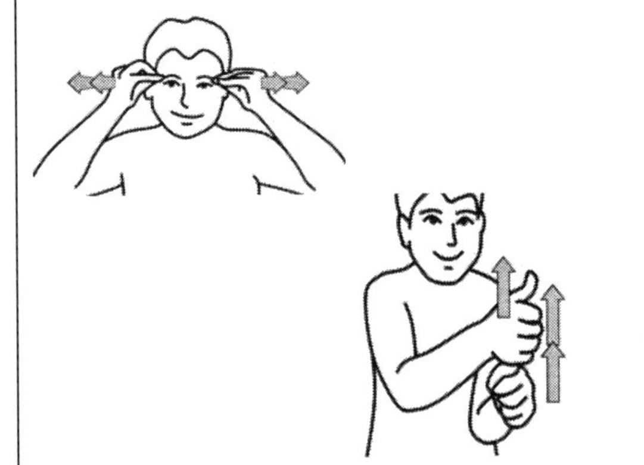
tickle - cosquilla Wiggle the fingers of both curved "5" hands in front of each shoulder. Indicates the act of tickling a person.	
tired – cansado(a) Fingertips of the bent hands are placed at each side of the body just inside the shoulders and then dropped slightly. Indicates the shoulders falling forward when tired. [also: weary, exhausted]	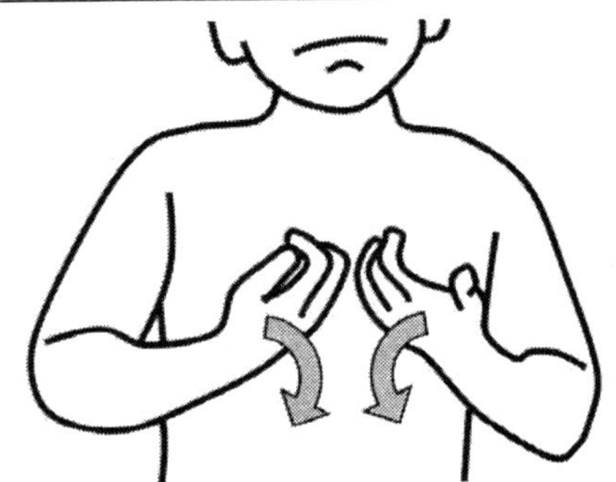
under – abajo de, debajo de Move the dominant "A" hand under the open reference hand, palm facing down. Indicates being under something else.	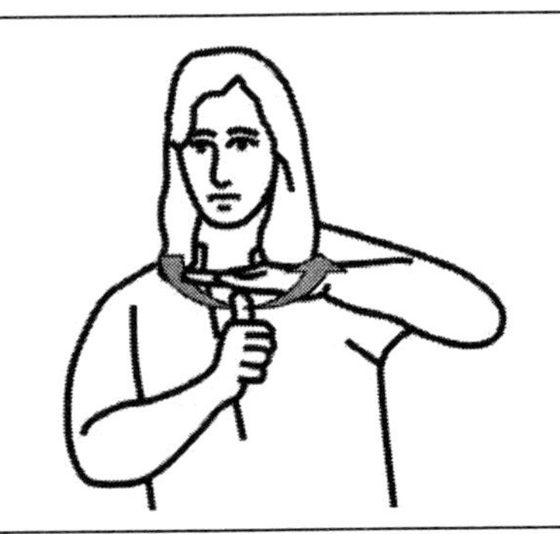

worm – gusano, lombriz Make the dominant bent index finger, palm facing forward, inch forward against the palm of the reference hand, palm facing dominant side, as it wiggles. Indicates a worm inching along.	

ACTIVITIES

- Cooking activities (cut off cookies, say utensils 1st, then, next)
- Board Games – Cards – Dominos. All with simple rules.
- Books!!!! – Especially those with repeating and rhyming phrases.
- Counting games (drop in the bucket, barrel full of monkeys)
- Play who/what games
- Cut and pasting activities using shapes – Sponge painting -- make a collage from magazine cutouts.
- Dramatic Play – Different occupations/jobs – Lot's of language opportunities.
- Make a huge tent with blanket and chairs and talk about what is in the woods. Pretend you're all on a far away planet and tell what it's like in this strange, new place.
- Simon Says (2 actions), Mother May I? Red Light Green Light
- Rhyming games
- Texture bag
- Grab bag – Add story-building game as your child guesses what the object is or what it's used for.
- Treasure Hunt – Scavenger Hunt

43 to 48 Months

DEVELOPMENTAL MILESTONES

- Speech is more fluid and understandable
- Uses up to 1,000 – 1,500 words
- Comprehends up to 1,500 – 2,000 words
- Begins to understand the difference between fiction/non-fiction
- Uses more details in conversation
- Emerging ability to accurately discuss topics/events, e.g. "out of context"
- Effectively uses vocabulary to express personal thoughts – discusses emotions and feelings
- Narrative and retelling skills – able to tell and sequence story or situation events, emerging understanding of characters and character development
- Emerging use of conjunctions – "because"
- Emerging use of reflexive pronouns – "myself"

SIGNS

clouds	head	pig	sheep
cake	home	reading	sun
delicious	nap-time	run	thunder
elephant	pie	share	

43-48 MONTHS SIGNS (ENGLISH/SPANISH)

cloud(s) - nube

Begin with both "C" hands near the reference side of the head, palms facing each other, bring the hands away from each other in outward arcs while turning the palms in. Repeat near the dominant side of the head.

Shape and location of clouds.

cake - pastel

Beginning with the fingertips of the curved dominant "5" hand on the palm of the reference open hand, raise the dominant hand upward.

Indicates a cake rising.

delicious - delicioso

Touch the bent middle finger of the dominant 5 hand to the lips, palm facing in, and then twist the dominant hand quickly forward.

elephant - elefante

Starting with the bent open hand at the nose, fingers pointing forward and palm down, swoop the hand downward, ending forward movement at the chest level.

Indicates an elephant's trunk.

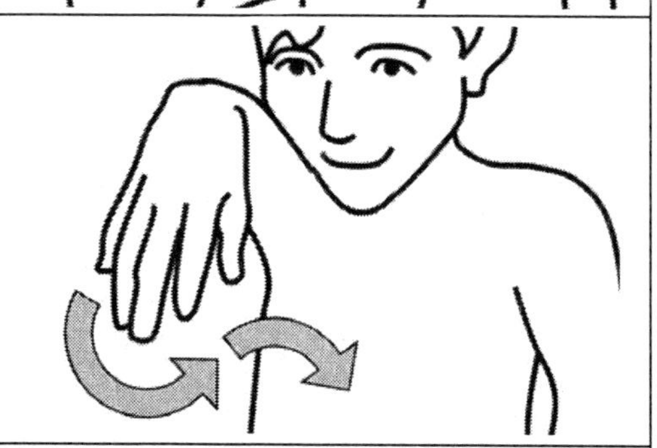

head - cabeza

Place the fingertips of the dominant bent hand against the same-sided temple and then move the dominant hand downward in an arc to the jaw.

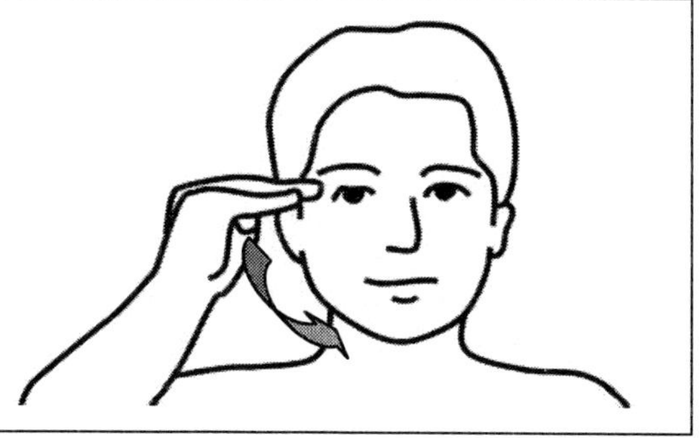

home – hogar, casa

Place the tips of the "flat O" hand against the mouth and then the cheek (or, place the flat hand on the cheek.)

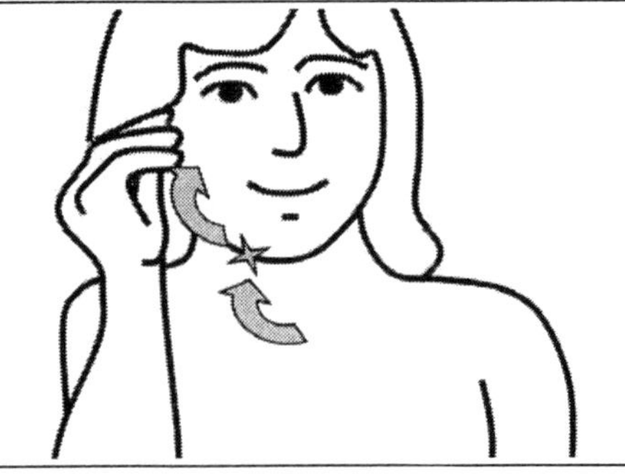

nap-time – siesta, sueñecito

Place the slightly curved dominant hand on the dominant cheek and tilt the head to the dominant side.

As if laying down your head on the hand.

[also: bed]

pie – pastel, torta

Slide the fingertips of the dominant open hand, palm facing reference, from the fingers to the heel of the upturned reference hand, fingers pointing forward, and then perpendicularly across the reference palm.

Indicates cutting a pie into slices.

[Can also be used with a "C" hand for cake]

pig – cerdo, puerco

With the back of the dominant open hand, under the chin, palm facing down, bend the dominant fingers down, and then up again with a double movement.

read - leer

Move the fingertips of the dominant "V" hand, palm facing down, from the thumb to the little finger of the reference open hand.

Indicates the movement of the eyes down a page to read it.

run - correr

Hook the index of the dominant "L" under the thumb of the reference "L" and move the hands forward in a quick short motion.

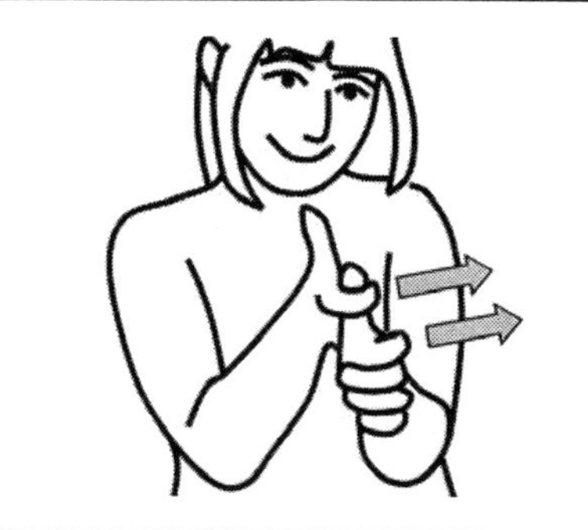

share – compartir, participar

Open dominant hand is placed in the crook of the open reference hand and moves back and forth as if cutting a portion of something to share.

As if cutting a portion.

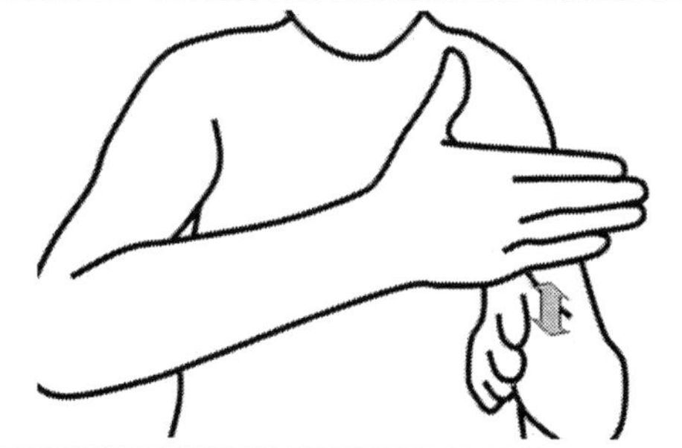

sheep - oveja

Slide the back of the fingers of the dominant "V" hand, palm facing up from the wrist up the inside of the forearm of the reference bent arm with a short repeated movement.

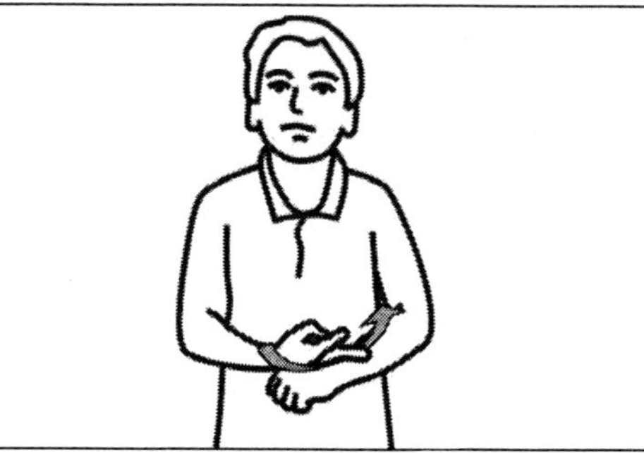

sun - sol

The "C"' hand is held at the dominant temple and extended forward and upward.

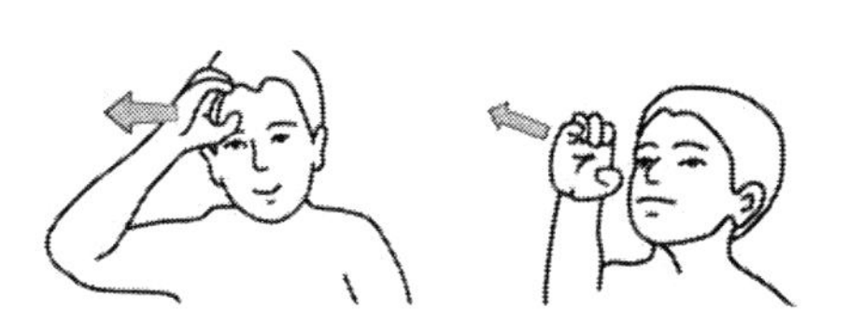

thunder – trueno, tronar

Touch the extended dominant index finger to the dominant ear. Then shake both "S" hands from side to side with a repeated movement in front of each shoulder.

ACTIVITIES

- Daily schedule – Sequence events – Routine activities
- "What if….." stories. Support descriptive language use and problem solving skills – "If my ice cream fell off the cone, I would feel _______. But, then I could _________" Include opportunities for "fact" or "fable" stories. "If I were King, I would …… Then, I would….."
- Turn taking stories – Build on from one day to the next. Supports comprehension and retention/retelling skills.
- Dressing self dolls…buttons, Velcro, undergarments, ties
- Simon Says (3 actions)
- Nature hunt – explore ponds, back yard, trails, etc.
- Petting farms – Age-appropriate plays, concerts, fairs, etc
- Circle games
- Drama activities for children

49 to 60 Months

DEVELOPMENTAL MILESTONES

- Connected speech and language understandable
- Uses "what do…does…did" questions
- Uses 1,500 to 2,000 words
- Answers simple "when" questions
- Retells long story with increasing accuracy
- Knows and can state full name – first, middle, last
- Reflexive pronouns emerging more consistently
- Comparatives vs. superlatives emerging – "-er," "-est"
- Uses 5 to 8 word sentences
- Developing understanding of prepositions – between, above, below, bottom
- Repeats the days of the week
- Emerging ability to name months – knows birthday (day and month)

SIGNS

baseball
catch
dirty
dream
go
grandmother
grandfather
hug
say
soccer
welcome
Monday
Tuesday
Wednesday
Thursday
Friday
Saturday
Sunday

baseball - béisbol

With the little finger of the dominant "S" hand on the index finger of the reference "S" hand, palms facing in opposite directions, move the hands from near the dominant shoulder downward in an arc across the front of the body.

Natural gesture of swinging a baseball bat.

catch, coger, agarrar

Move the dominant curved hand into the reference curved "5" hand in front of the chest.

Indicates receiving a ball into a glove.

dirty – sucio, cochino

With the back of the dominant open hand, under the chin, palm facing down, wiggle the fingers.

dream - sueño

Move the extended dominant index finger from the dominant side of the forehead, outward and upward to the dominant hand while bending the finger up and down.

Indicates an image coming from the mind.

go – irse, marchar, andar

Begin with both hands raised in front of the chest with the index finger pointing up, then move both hands simultaneously to the reference side in a downward arc movement.

grandfather - abuelo Sign "father". Place the thumb of the dominant "5" hand on the forehead. then bounce forward from forehead once. Origin: One generation away from father.	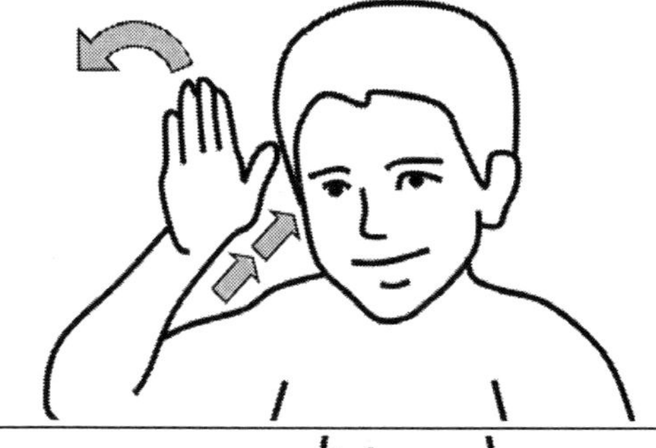
grandmother - abuela Sign "mother". Place the thumb of the "5" hand on the chin, then bounce forward once. Origin: One generation away from mother.	
hug - abrazo The hands hold the upper arms as if hugging yourself.	
say – dicho, decir, aserto The index finger, held in front of the mouth, moves forward towards the person being addressed. [also: speak, say, tell, speech]	
soccer - fútbol Flick the index finger of the dominant hand on the open palm of the reference hand.	 

welcome – bienvenido(a) Bring the upturned dominant curved hand from in front of the dominant side of the body in toward the center of the waist. **You are welcome – de nada**	
Monday - Lunes [Initialized sign] Move the dominant "M" hand, palm facing in, in a double circle in front of the dominant shoulder.	
Tuesday - Martes [Initialized sign] Move the dominant "T" hand, palm facing in, in a circle in front of the dominant shoulder.	
Wednesday - Miércoles [Initialize sign] Move the dominant "W" hand, palm facing out and fingers pointing up, in a circle in front of the dominant shoulder.	
Thursday - Jueves [Abbreviation "T" + "H"] Beginning with the dominant "T" hand in front of the dominant shoulder, palm facing forward in a small circle, quickly switch to the "H" hand and continue the circle.	

Friday - Viernes [Initialized sign] Move the dominant "F" hand, palm facing in, in a repeated circle in front of the dominant shoulder.	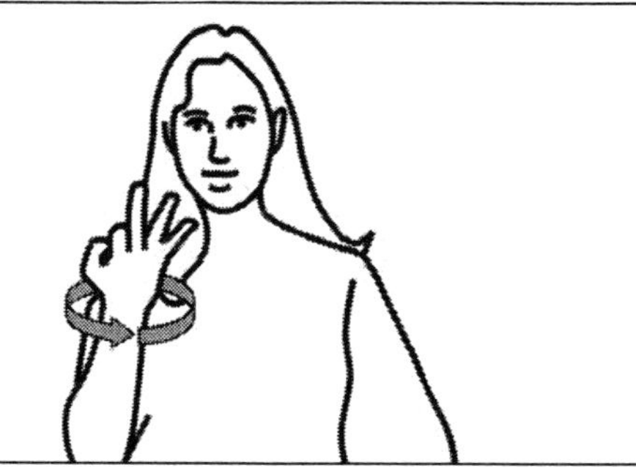
Saturday - Sábado [Initialized sign] Move the dominant "S" hand, palm facing out, in a small circle in front of the dominant shoulder.	
Sunday - Domingo [The movement of the hands shows reverence and awe] Beginning with both open hands in front of each shoulder, palms facing forward and fingers pointing up, move the hands forward in small inward circles.	

ACTIVITIES

- Big/bigger/biggest comparison games
- Dominoes, board games, card games – with increasing number of rules and complexity
- Puzzles and building blocks – More complex – smaller pieces – larger number of pieces, etc. 3-D puzzles are great – Your help playing and putting things together is an essential part of supporting your child's schema building – problem solving and higher level thinking, etc.
- What's missing? – What did I take away? Games with cards, or silly/ordinary objects.
- What's wrong with this picture? Supports connection between cognitive and language building skills.
- Advanced concentration/memory games
- Make a calendar – or Daily Routine Chart
- Pretend play with money – store scenarios that build basic money concepts and mathematical reasoning skills. "If you have 10 cents, you could have….." (10 pennies, or 2 nickels, or 5 pennies and 1 nickel, or 1 dime), etc. Make change using quarters only or quarters and dollar bills. To add to the fun make your own pretend money – Put your own picture on the coins!

SIGNS

ALPHABET HAND SHAPES

Aa		Gg	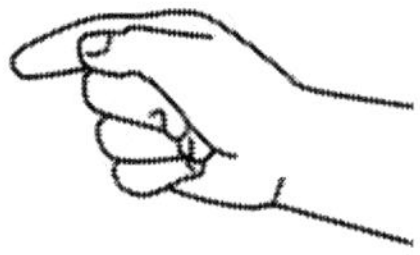
Bb	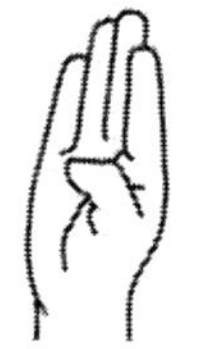	Hh	
Cc		Ii	
Dd		Jj	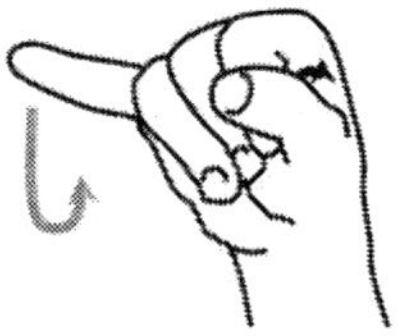
Ee		Kk	
Ff	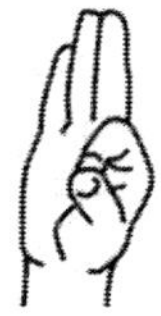	Ll	

ALPHABET HAND SHAPES

Mm		Tt	
Nn		Uu	
Oo		Vv	
Pp		Ww	
Qq		Xx	
Rr		Yy	
Ss		Zz	

NUMBER HAND SHAPES (ENGLISH/SPANISH)

0 zero-cero	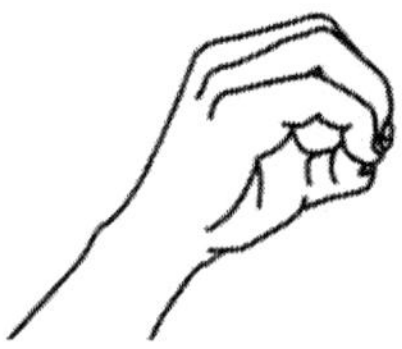	6 six-seis	
1 one-uno		7 seven-siete	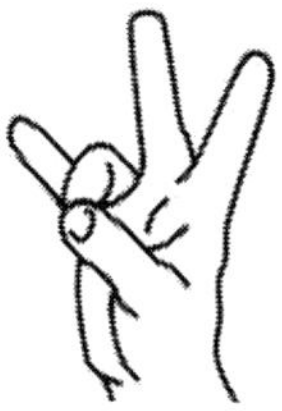
2 two-dos	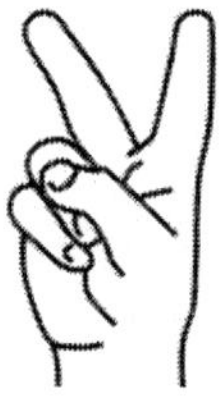	8 eight-ocho	
3 three-tres		9 nine-nueve	
4 four-cuatro		10 ten-diez	
5 five-cinco			

airplane – aeroplano, avión

Use the "Y" hand, with index finger extended and palm facing down. Make forward upward sweeping motion.

As if flying an airplane across the sky.

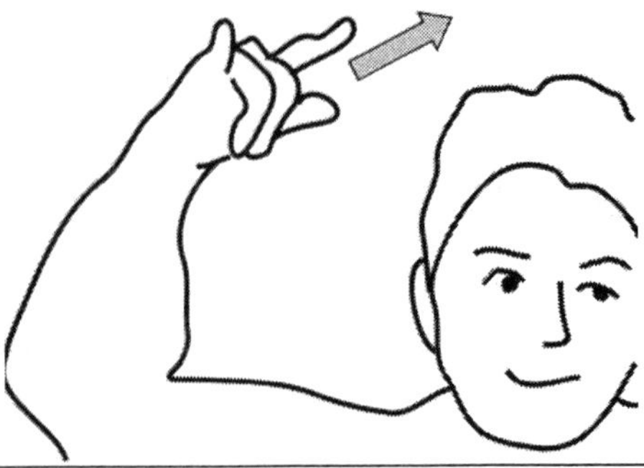

apple - manzana

With the knuckle of the bent index finger on the dominant cheek, twist downward.

baby – criatura, bebé

Place the dominant hand in the crook of the reference hand and make a gentle rocking motion from side to side.

As if cradling a baby in your arms.

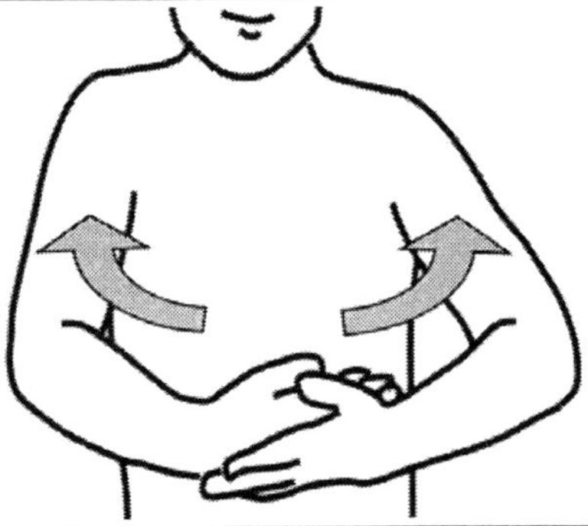

banana - plátano

Move the closed fingertips of the dominant hand, palm facing outward, down the extended reference index finger.

As if peeling your index finger.

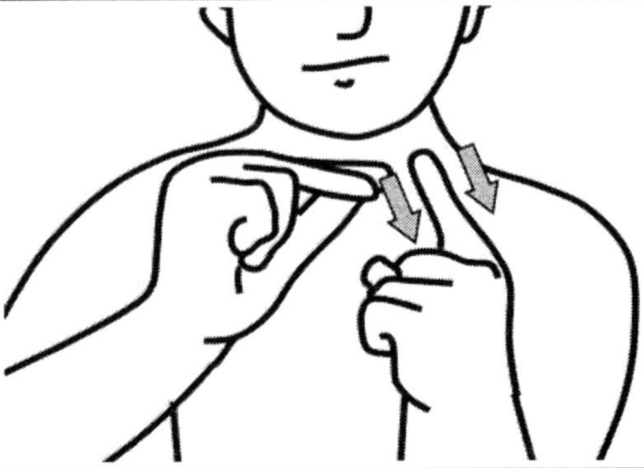

bath - baño

For wash rub the "A" hands together palm to palm.

For bath rub the "A" hands on the chest near the shoulder.

[also: scrub, wash]

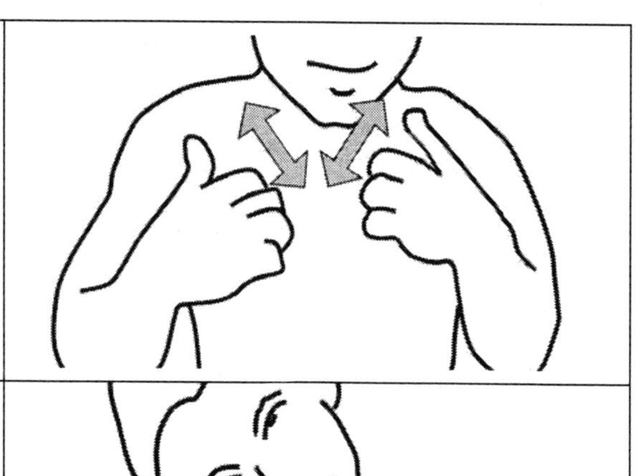

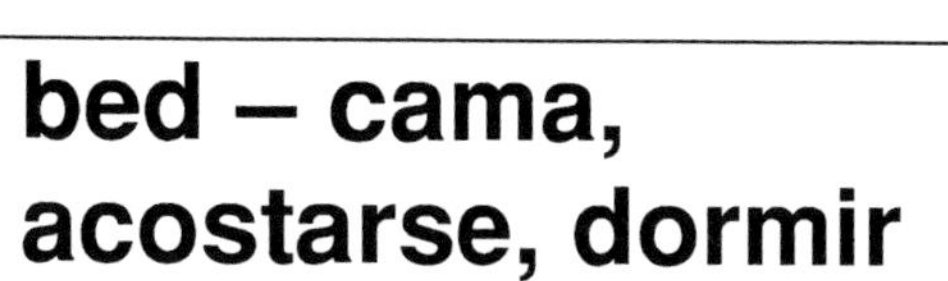

bed – cama, acostarse, dormir

Place the slightly curved dominant hand on the same-sided cheek and tilt the head to the side.

As if laying down your head on the hand.

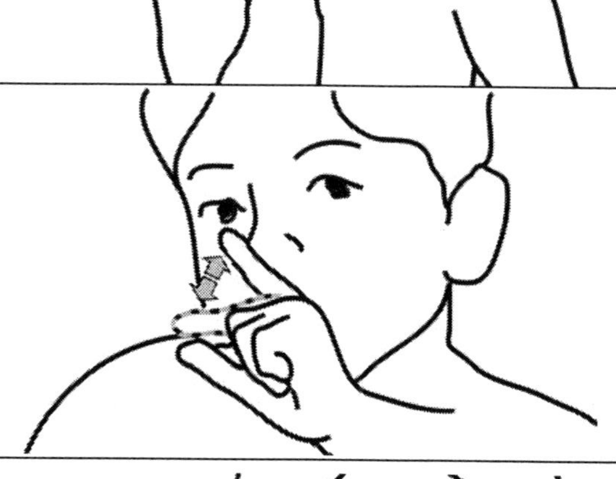

bird - pájaro

With the "g" hand at the mouth, palm forward, repeatedly open and close the index finger.

As if displaying a birds beak.

black - negro

Draw the index finger across the dominant eyebrow from reference to dominant.

blue - azul

Shake the dominant “B” hand in front of the chest.

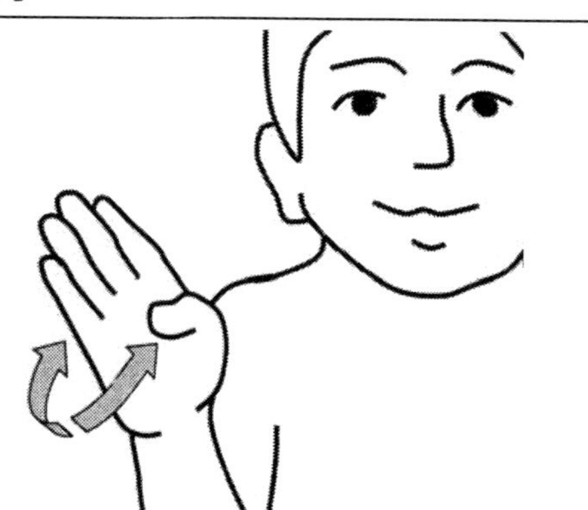

book - libro

Starting with both palms touching in front of the chest, fingers pointing forward, move the hands apart, keeping the little fingers together.

As if opening a book.

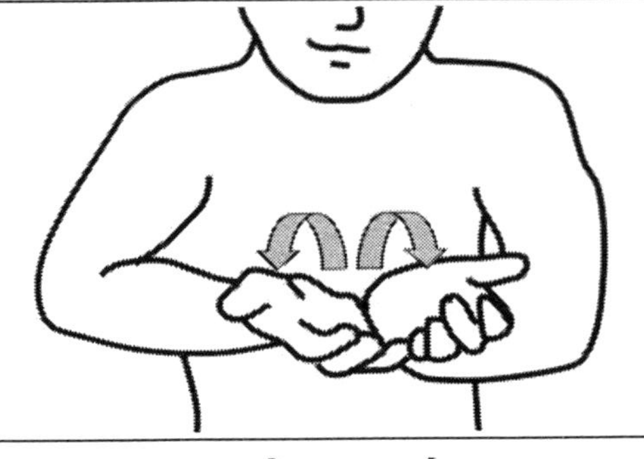

bottle - botella

The reference open hand is held palm up. The dominant "C" hand moves from on the reference hand up. As if holding a bottle in your hands.

[also: cup, glass]

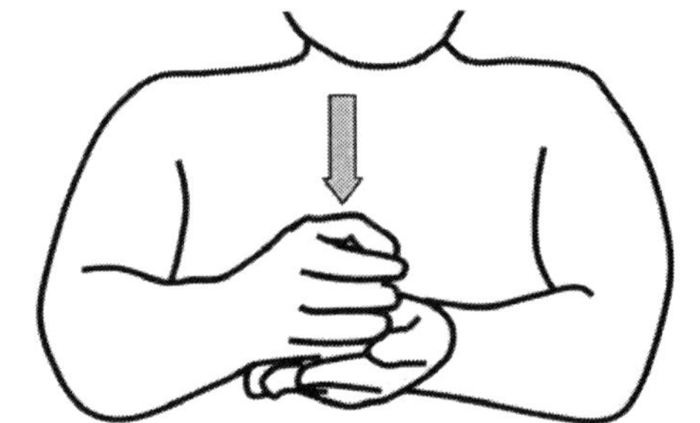

brown – moreno, café

Move the index-finger side of the dominant "B" hand down the cheek.

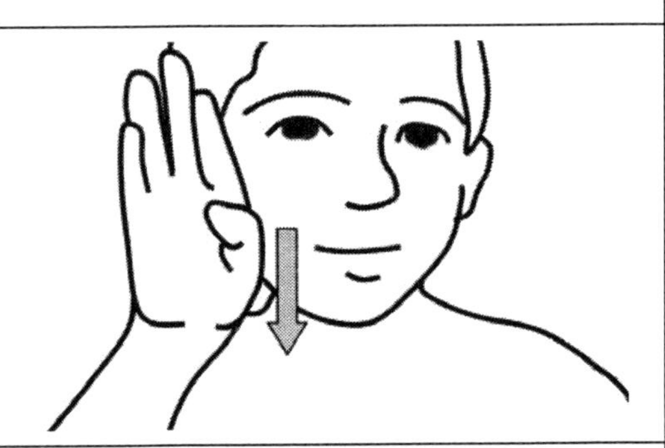

butterfly - mariposa

With the hands crossed at the wrist, palms toward the chest, and the thumbs of the open hands hooked together, flex and straighten several times.

As if demonstrating how a butterfly's wings flutter.

car - carro, coche, auto

Place the "S" hands in front of you, palms facing each other, and alternate clockwise then counter- clockwise as if driving a car.

As if steering a car.

[also: automobile, drive]

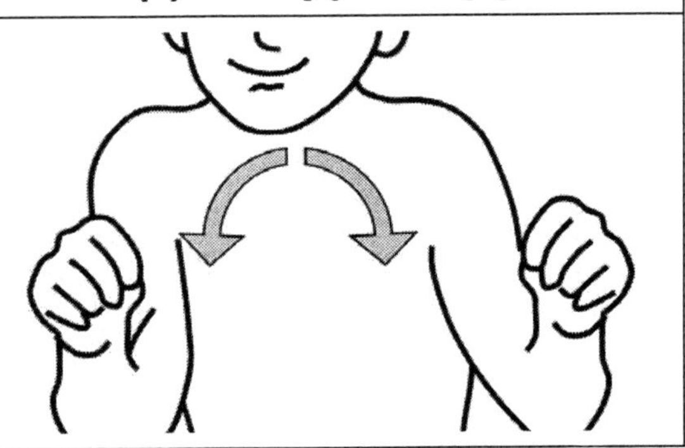

cat – gato(a)

The "F" hand touches the corner of the upper lip, brushing out and away from the face a couple of times.

As if you are stroking a cat's whiskers.

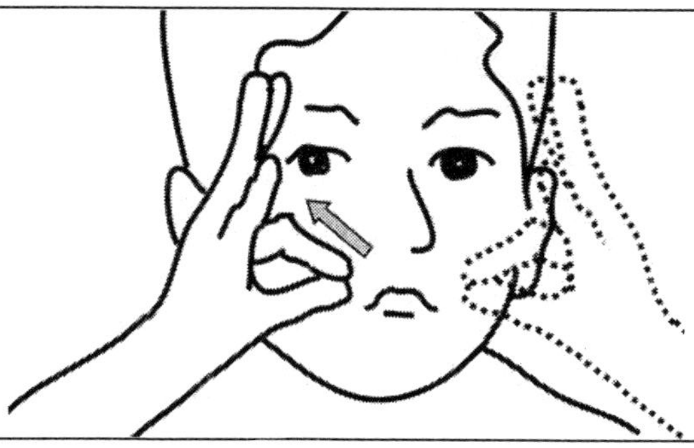

change - cambio

With both modified "X" hands, place the dominant "X" so the palm faces forward, with the reference "X" facing it. Twist the hands around until they have reversed positions.

[also: adjust, adapt]

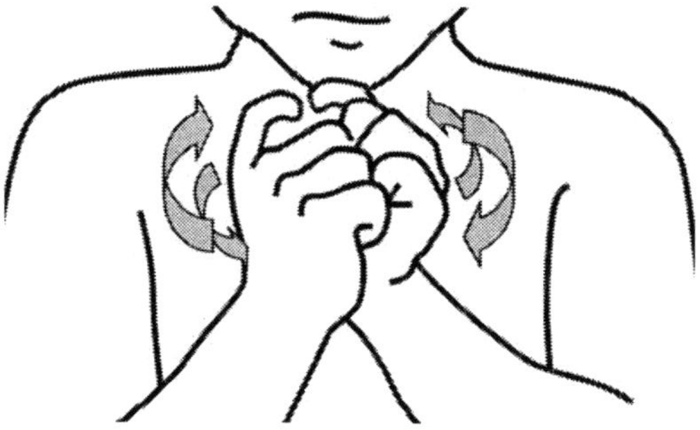

cold - frío

Shake both "S" hands, palms facing each other.

Indicating cold, "Brr!"

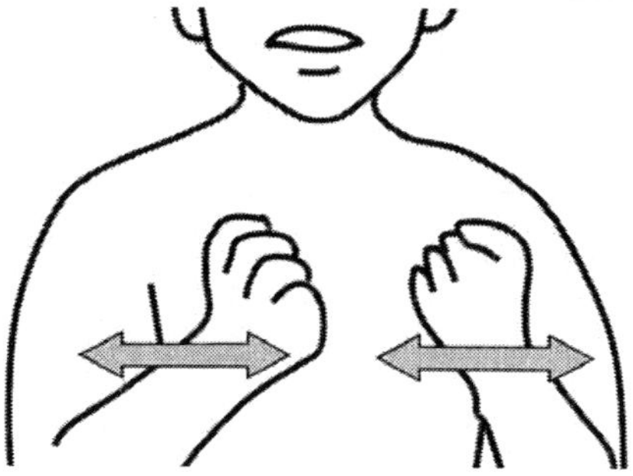

colors – colores, color

Place the "5" hand in front of the mouth and wiggle the fingers as the hand moves away slightly.

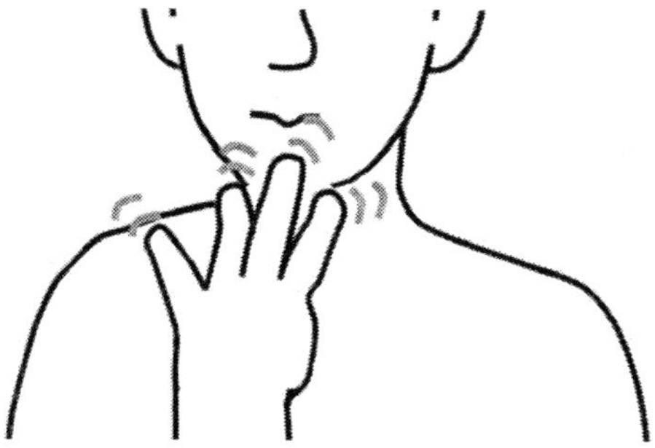

cookie - galleta

Touch the fingers of the dominant clawed "5" hand on the upturned reference palm and then twist the dominant hand and touch the reference palm again.

As if cutting cookies with a cookie cutter.

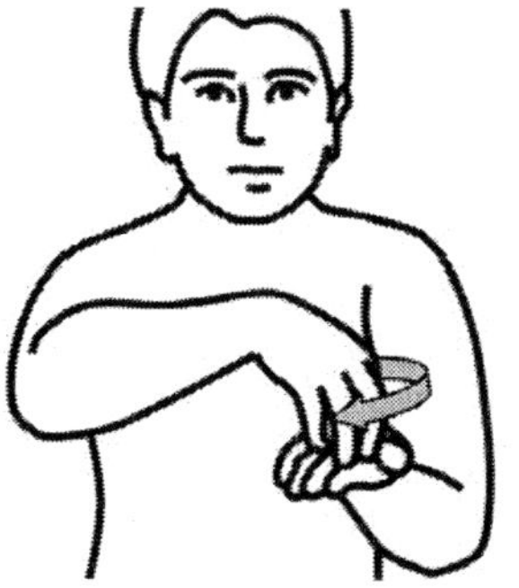

dog - perro

Snap the middle finger against the thumb. Can also add slapping the upper leg.

As if calling a dog.

down - abajo

Point down with the index finger.

drink – bebida, tomar, beber

Use the "c" hand in front of the mouth and thumb touching bottom lip; then keeping the thumb in place, move fingers upward toward the nose.

As if taking a drink with the hands.

earache – dolor de oidos

Jab both index fingers toward each other several times in front of ear.

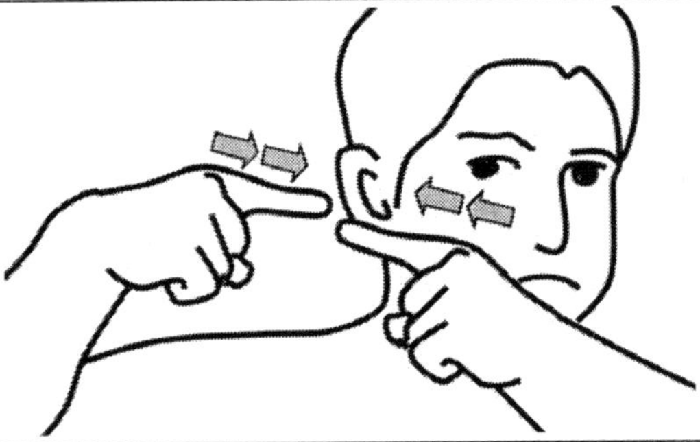

eat - comer

With the thumb and fingertips together, palm facing down, repeatedly move the fingertips towards the lip with short movements.

As if putting food in ones mouth.

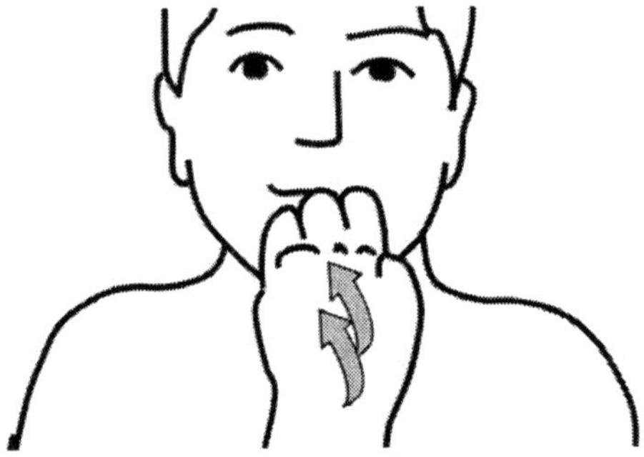

father - padre
Place the thumb of the dominant "5" hand on the forehead.

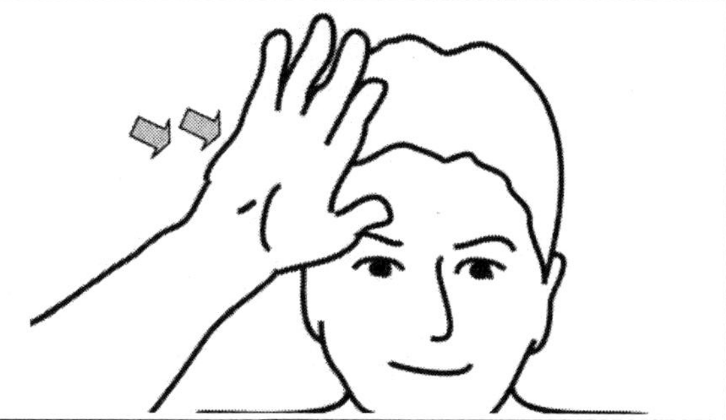

fish - pez
Begin with the dominant open hand palm facing the reference side and the reference extended index finger on the heel of the dominant hand. Swing the dominant hand back and forth with a double movement.

Like a fish swimming.

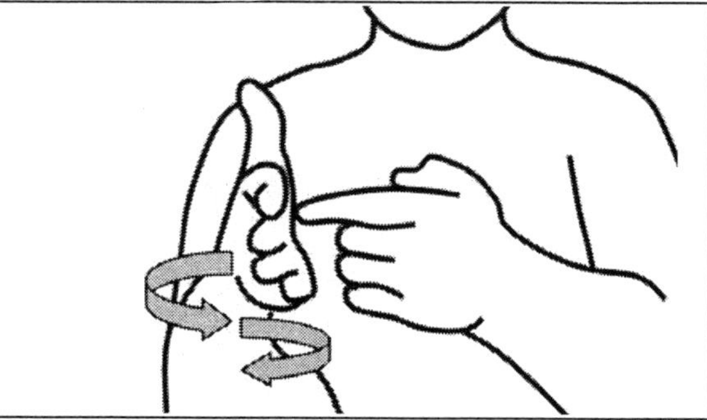

flower - flor
First place the tips of the "flat O" hand first under one nostril, then under the other.

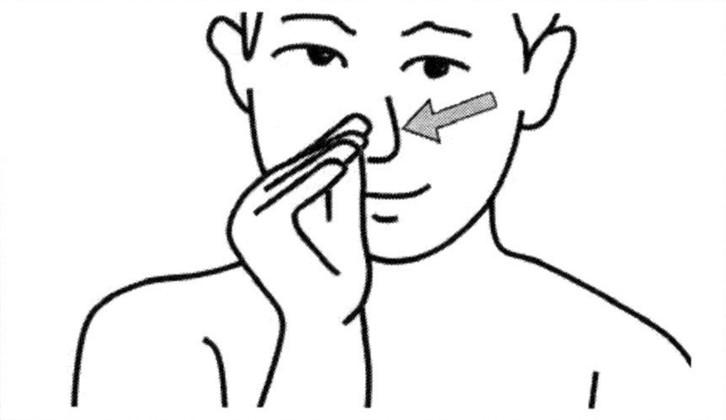

friend – amigo(a)
Interlock dominant "X" hand index finger down over upturned reference "X" hand index finger.

Indicates holding hands with someone.

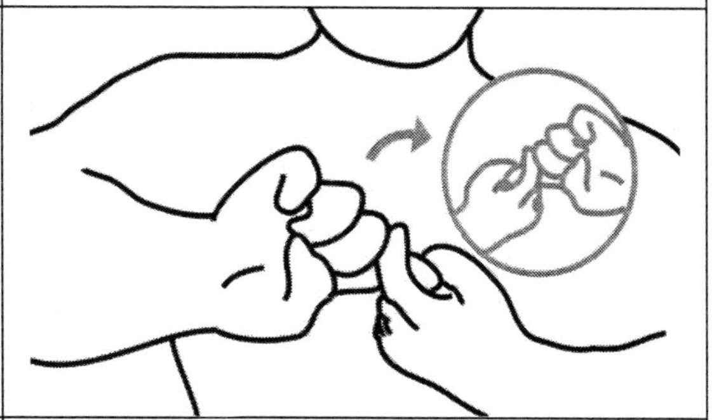

good – bien, bueno(a)
Starting with fingertips of the open hand on the lips, move the hand away and down from the mouth to touch the open palm.

Indicates something tasted good and you want more.

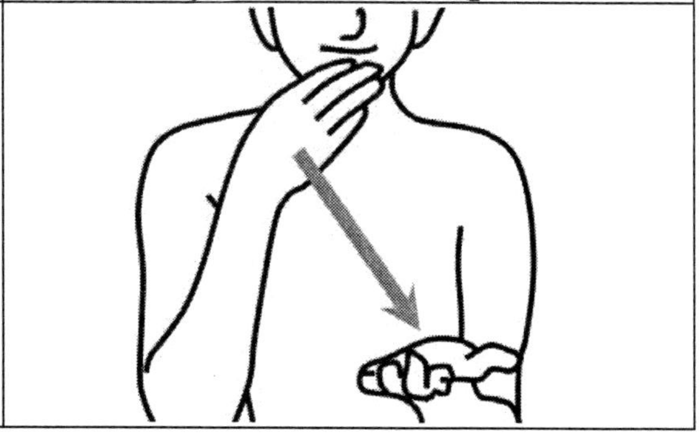

green - verde

Shake the dominant "G" handshape in front of the chest.

happy – feliz, alegre, contento

The open hands pat the chest several times with a slight upward motion.

As if heart is pounding with joy.

[also: glad, rejoice, joy]

head - cabeza

Place the fingertips of the dominant bent hand against the same-sided temple and then move the dominant hand downward in an arc to the jaw.

hear – oir, escuchar

Point the index finger towards the ear.

As if showing the ear to listen.

[also: ear]

help - ayuda

Place the dominant open hand under the reference "A" hand, thumb up, lift both hands together.

[also: aid, assist]

hot - caliente Place the dominant "C" hand at the mouth, palm facing in; give the wrist a quick twist, so the palm faces out. [also: heat]	
hug – abrazo, abrazar The hands hold the upper arms as if hugging yourself.	
love- amor, cariño The "S" hands are crossed at the wrist and pressed to the heart. As if hugging one's self.	
milk - leche With the "C" hand in front of the body, palm reference and fingers forward, close the hand to an "S" shape, repeatedly. As if milking a cow.	
mine - mío Place the dominant open hand on the chest.	

moon - luna

Tap the thumb of the modified "C" hand over the dominant eye, palm facing forward, with a double movement.

The symbol represents the crescent moon.

more - más

Bring the tips of both "flat O" hands together, pop together 2 times.

mother - madre

Place the thumb of the “5” hand on the chin.

no - no

Bring the index, middle finger, and thumb together in one motion.

orange – naranja

Squeeze the "S" hand once or twice at the chin. Sign for the color the fruit.

[Same sign for color or fruit]

orange – anaranjado

Squeeze the "S" hand once or twice at the chin. Sign for the color orange.

pain - dolor The index fingers are jabbed toward each other several times. [also: pain, ache]	
please – por favor Rub the chest with the open hand in a circular motion (palm facing yourself) As if rubbing your heart. [also: pleasure, enjoy, like]	
purple – púrpura, morado Gently shake the fingers of the "P" handshape.	
rain - lluvia Let both curved "5" hands, palms facing down, drop down several times in short, quick motions.	
rainbow – arco iris Make a large arc from the reference to the dominant as indicated by the arrows, while wiggling fingers.	

red - rojo
Move the inside tip of the dominant index finger down across the lips. Also, made with an "R" handshape.

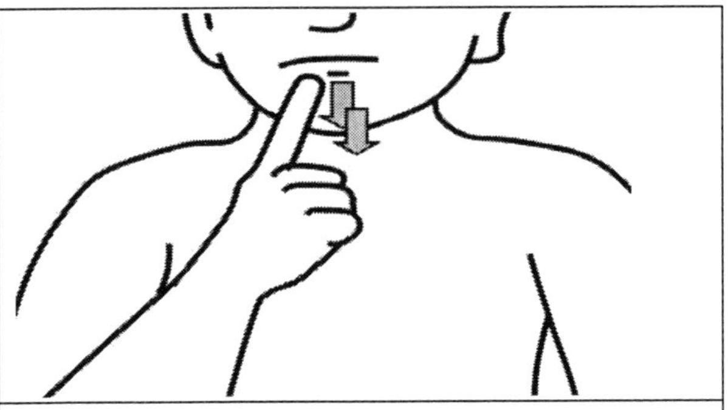

shoes - zapatos
Strike the sides of the "S" hands together several times.

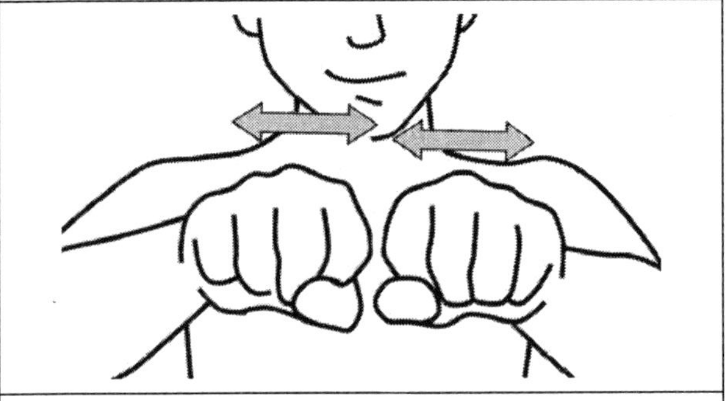

sleepy – soñoliento, dormido
Lie the side of head on the dominant hand.

Indicates sleeping on pillow.

socks - calcetín
Place the index fingers side-by-side and rub them back and forth several times, tilting downwards.

As if two knitting needles are making socks.

[also: stockings, hose]

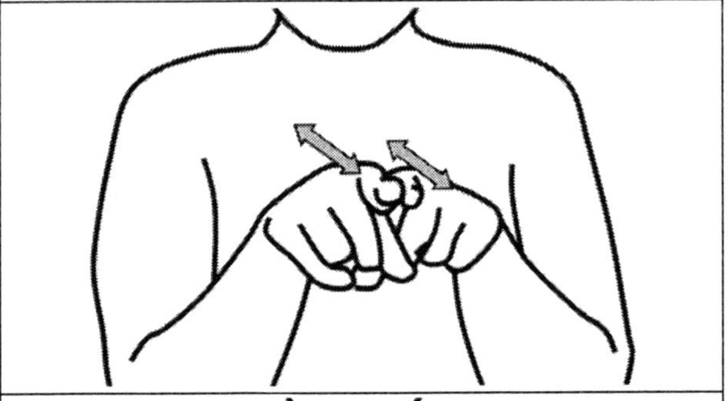

stop – parar, alto, detener, poner fin
Bring the little finger side of the dominant open hand abruptly down on the upturned reference palm.

As if chopping on something.

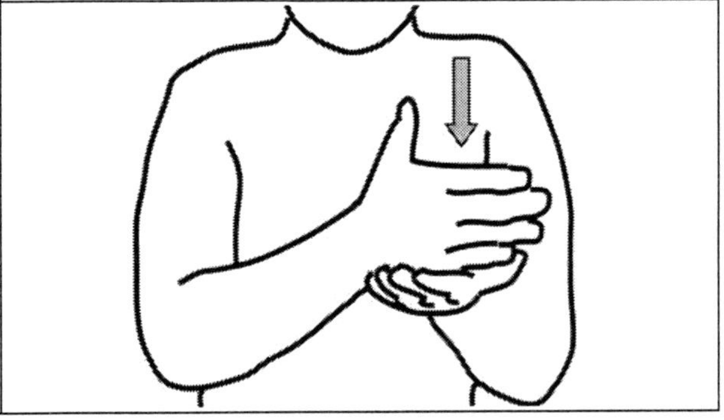

telephone - telefono

Place the thumb of the "Y" hand on the ear and the little finger at the mouth.

As if talking on the phone.

[also: call]

thank you - gracias

Touch lips with the fingertips of flat hand, then move the hand forward until the palm is facing up and towards the indicated person. Smile and nod head while doing this sign.

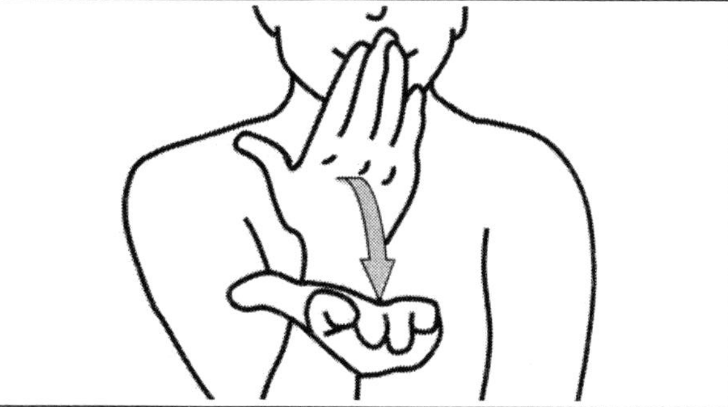

toilet – tocador, cuarto de baño, inodoro

Shake the dominant "T" hand from side to side in front of the body, palm facing forward.

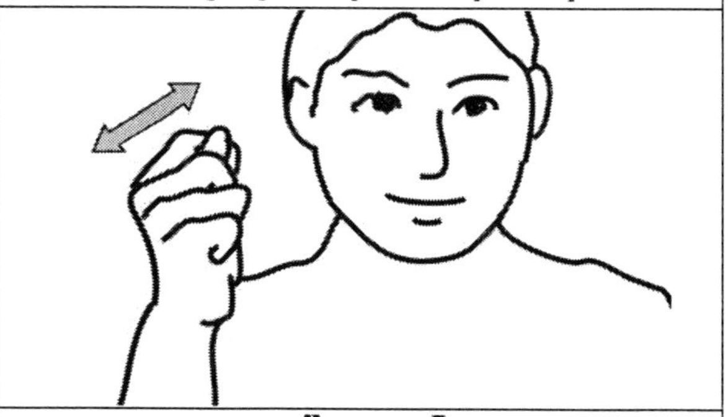

touch – tocar, toque

Touch the back of the reference hand with the dominant middle finger, other fingers extended.

Senses – touch - tacto

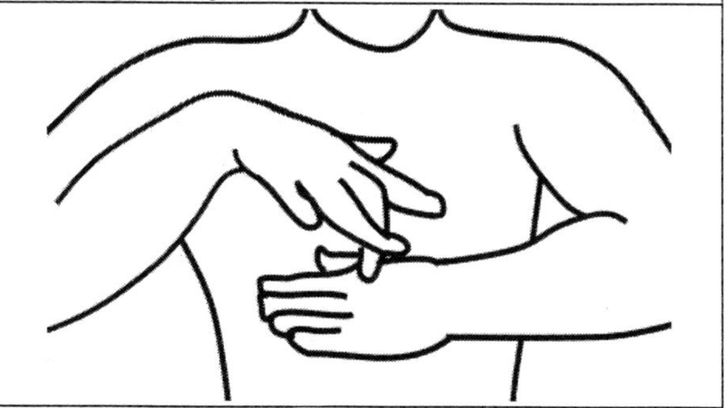

up – hacia arriba

Point up with the index finger of the dominant hand.

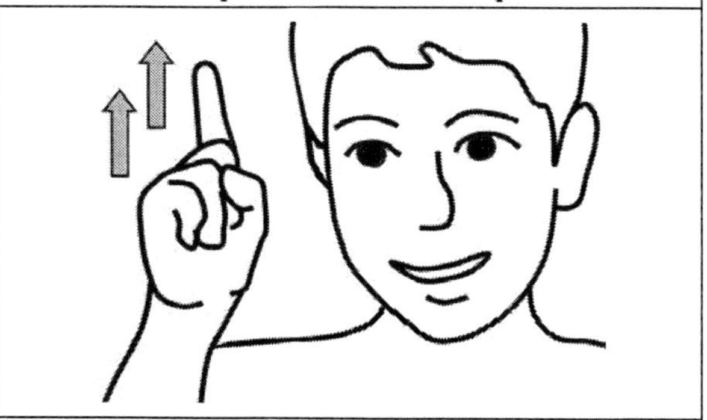

wait – esperar, espera Beginning with both curved "5" hands in front of the body, reference palm up in front of the dominant palm up, wiggle the fingers. As if asking for something.	
want – necesitar, querer Place both "curved 5" hands in front of you, palms up, and draw them towards you. As if gesturing to bring something to you.	
water - agua Touch the mouth with the index finger of the "W" hand a few times.	
where - dónde Hold up the dominant index finger and shake the hand back and forth quickly from reference to dominant.	
white - blanco Place fingertips of the "5" hand on the chest and move the hand forward into the flattened "O" hand.	

wood – madera, leña Slide the little finger side of the dominant open hand, palm facing reference and fingers pointing forward, back and forth with a double movement across the index finger side of the reference open hand, palm facing in.	
yellow - amarillo Gently shake the "Y" handshape at chest level.	
yes - sí Shake the "S" hand up and down in front of you.	
yesterday - ayer Touch the dominant side of the cheek with the thumb of the dominant "Y" hand, and move in a semi-circle up and backwards towards the ear. The "A" hand can be used for this sign as well.	

change - cambio

With both modified "X" hands, place the dominant "X" so the palm faces forward, with the reference "X" facing it. Twist the hands around until they have reversed positions.

[also: adjust, adapt]

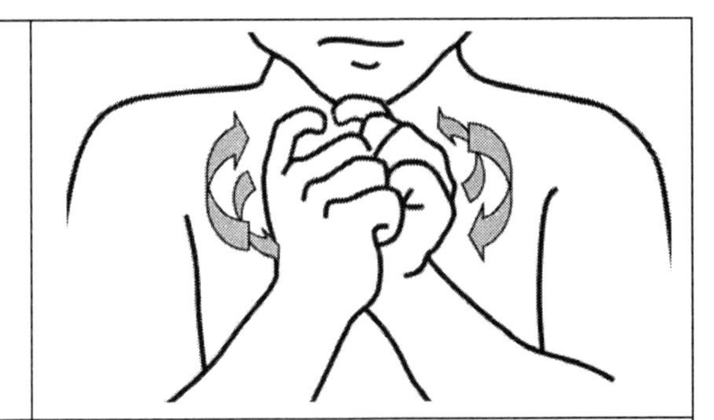

drink – bebida, tomar, beber

Use the "c" hand in front of the mouth and thumb touching bottom lip; then keeping the thumb in place, move fingers upward toward the nose.

As if taking a drink with the hands.

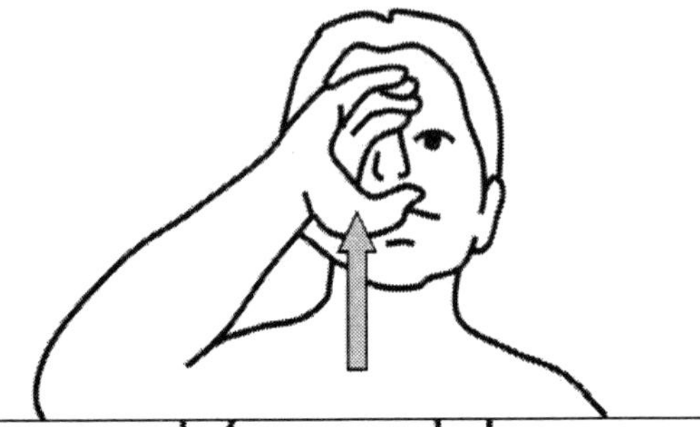

eat - comer

With the thumb and fingertips together, palm facing down, repeatedly move the fingertips towards the lip with short movements.

As if putting food in ones mouth.

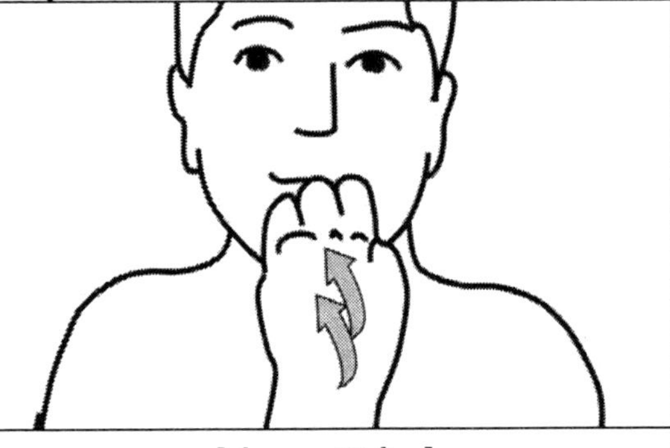

finish – fin, acabar

Hold the "5" hands in front of you, palms facing you, quickly twist hands to palms down.

[also: finished, completed, done, ended, over]

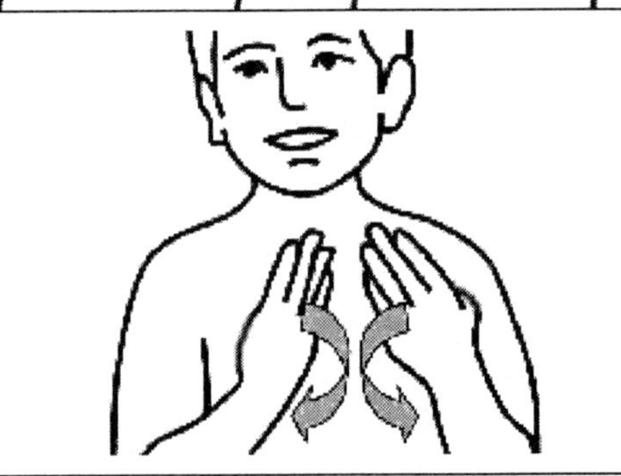

hear – oir, escuchar Point the index finger towards the ear. As if showing the ear to listen. [also: ear]	
help - ayuda Place the dominant open hand under the reference "A" hand, thumb up, lift both hands together. [also: aid, assist]	
hug – abrazo, abrazar The hands hold the upper arms as if hugging yourself.	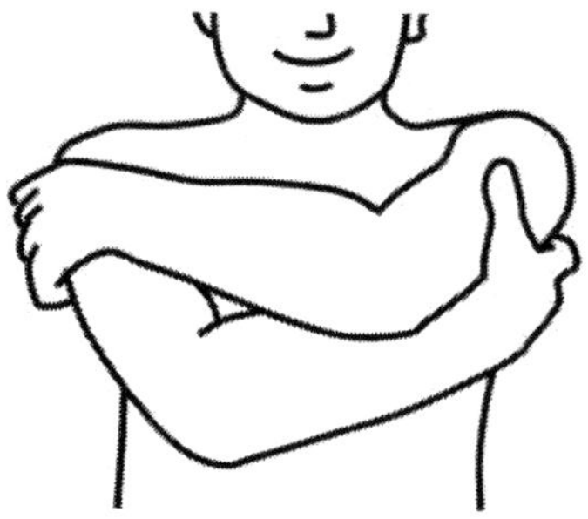
jump – salto, brinco Place the dominant "V" handshape in a standing position on the reference palm; lift the "V", bending the knuckles and return to a standing position.	
play – juego, jugar Place the "Y" hands in front of you and shake them in and out from the wrist a few times. [Play as in recreation]	

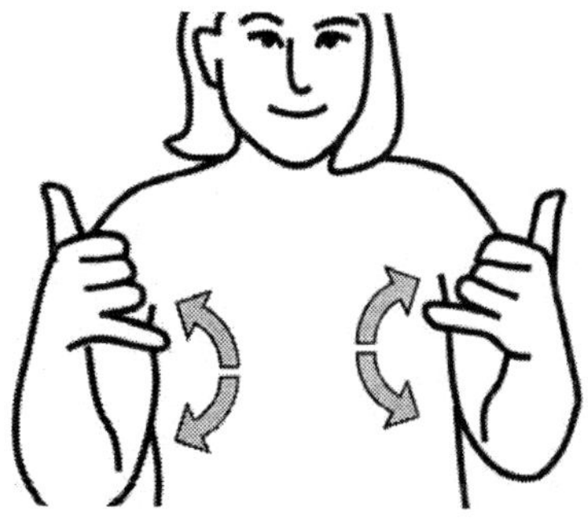

run – correr, carrera Hook the index of the dominant "L" under the thumb of the reference "L" and move the hands forward in a quick short motion.	
show – mostar, demostrar, enseñar Place the tip of the dominant index into the open reference hand, which is facing forward; and move both hands forward. [also reveal, for example]	
sleepy – soñoliento, dormido Move the open fingers down over the face into an "flat O" position near the chin, bowing the head slightly. Repeat.	
stop – parar, alto, detener, poner fin Bring the little finger side of the dominant open hand abruptly down on the upturned reference palm. As if chopping on something.	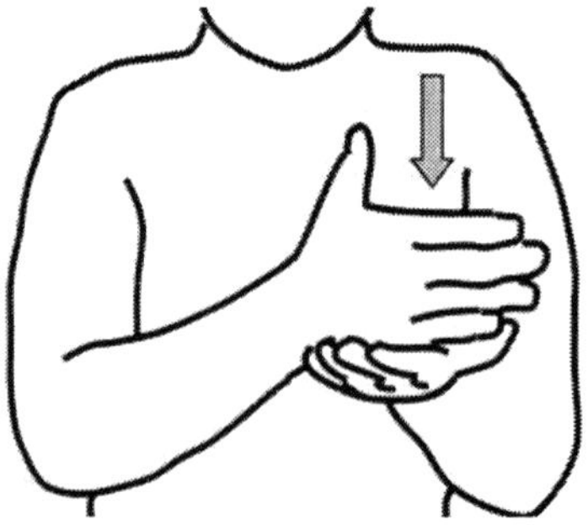
tell - decir The index finger, held in front of the mouth, rolls forward towards the person being addressed. [also speak, say, tell, speech]	

touch - tocar Touch the back of the reference hand with the dominant middle finger, other fingers extended. **Senses – touch - tacto**	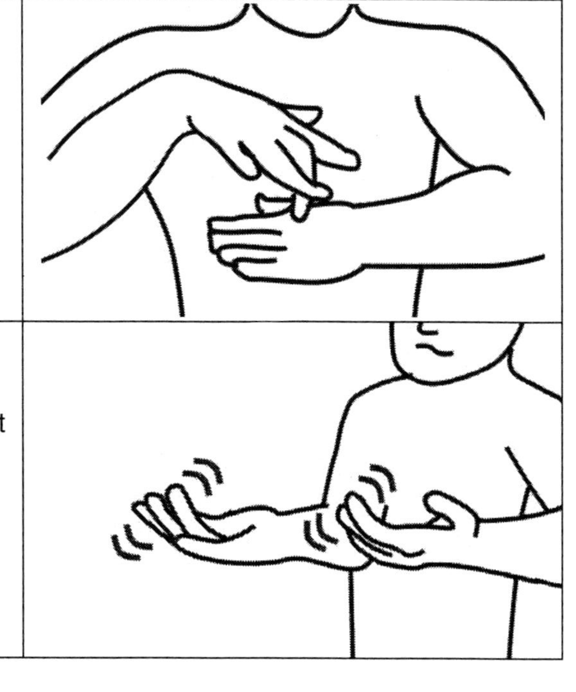
wait – esperar, espera Beginning with both curved "5" hands in front of the body, reference palm up in front of the dominant palm up, wiggle the fingers. As if asking for something.	

bear – oso(a)

Scratch the upper chest near the shoulders repeatedly with both "5" hands crossed in front of chest at the wrists.

As if giving a bear hug.

bee - obeja

Press the "F" hand against the dominant cheek. Then brush the index-finger side of the dominant "B" hand against the cheek.

Indicating the biting action of an insect then a natural gesture of brushing it away.

bird - pájaro

With the "g" hand at the mouth, palm forward, repeatedly open and close the index finger.

As if displaying a birds beak.

butterfly - mariposa

With the hands crossed at the wrist, palms toward the chest, and the thumbs of the open hands hooked together, flex and straighten several times.

As if demonstrating how a butterfly's wings flutter.

cat – gato(a)

The "F" hand touches the corner of the upper lip, brushing out and away from the face a couple of times.

As if you are stroking a cat's whiskers.

cow - vaca With the thumbs of the "Y" hands at the temples, bend the wrists forward a few times. Shows a cow's horns. As if showing a bull's horns.	
dog - perro Snap the middle finger against the thumb. Can also add slapping the upper leg. As if calling a dog.	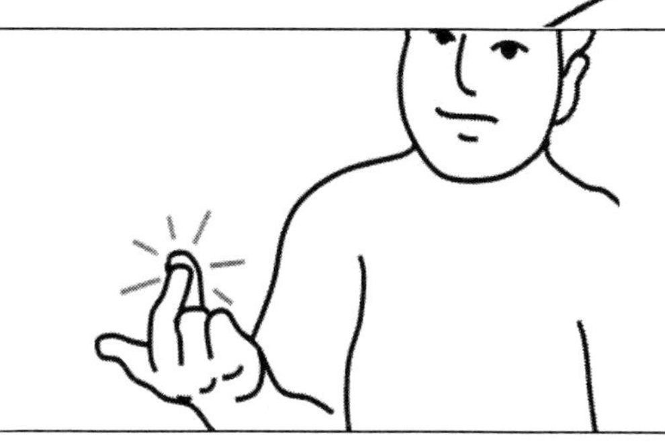
elephant - elefante Starting with the bent open hand at the nose, fingers pointing forward and palm down, swoop the hand downward, ending forward movement at the chest level. Indicates an elephant's trunk.	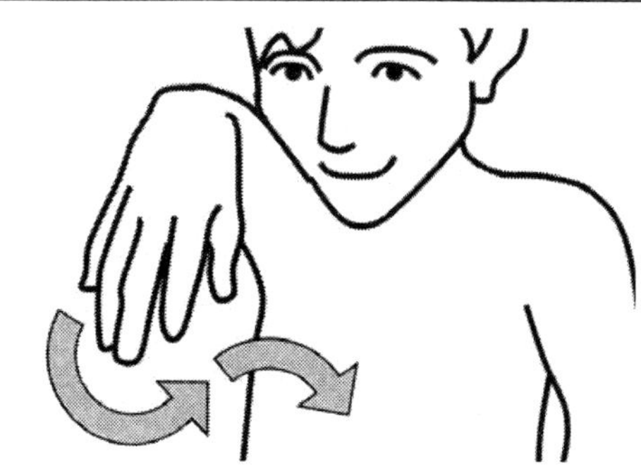
fish - pez Begin with the dominant open hand palm facing the reference side and the reference extended index finger on the heel of the dominant hand. Swing the dominant hand back and forth with a double movement. Like a fish swimming.	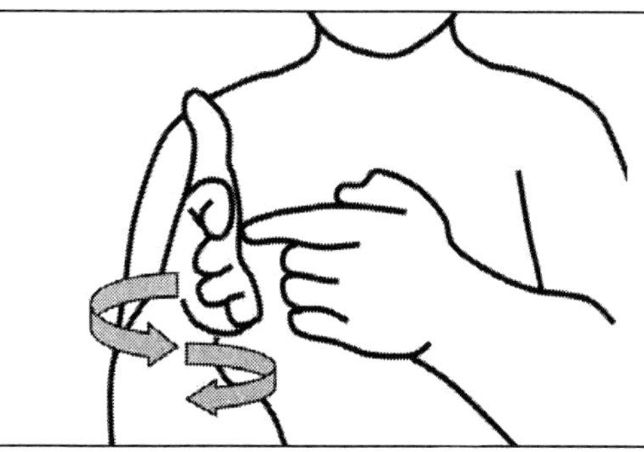
frog - rana Begin with "S" hand under the chin, flick the index and middle fingers outward. As if to indicate the filling of air into the frog's throat.	

horse - caballo With the "U" hand beside the temple, bend and unbend the index and middle fingers. Indicates a horse's ears.	
lion - león Beginning with the fingers of the dominant curved "5" hand pointing down over the forehead, move the hand back over the top of the head. Indicates the lions mane.	
monkey - mono Scratch the ribs on both sides of the body with the curved "5" hands. As if scratching characteristics of monkeys.	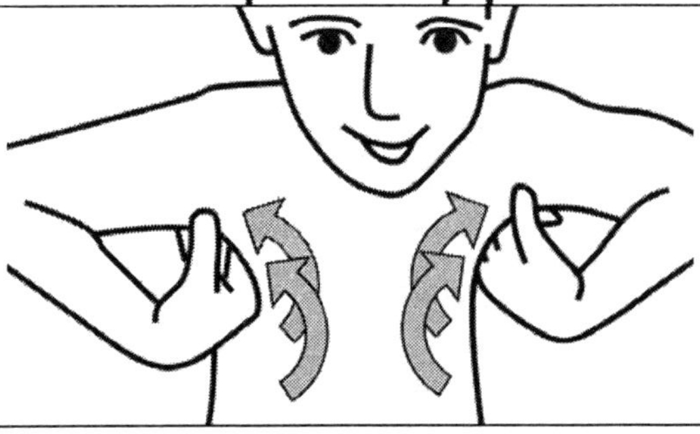
rabbit - conejo With the "U" hands crossed above the wrists, palms facing in and thumbs extended, bend the fingers of both hands forward and back towards the chest with a double movement. Indicates the rabbits ears.	
sheep - oveja Slide the back of the fingers of the dominant "V" hand, palm facing up from the wrist up the inside of the forearm of the reference bent arm with a short repeated movement.	

spider - araña With the hands crossed at the wrists, palms down, wriggle the fingers of both "claw" hands. Show the spider's legs crawling. Indicates the leg movement of a spider.	
tiger - tigre Move the fingertips of the "claw 5" hand from the cheeks outward, palms toward the face. As if showing the cheeks of a tiger .	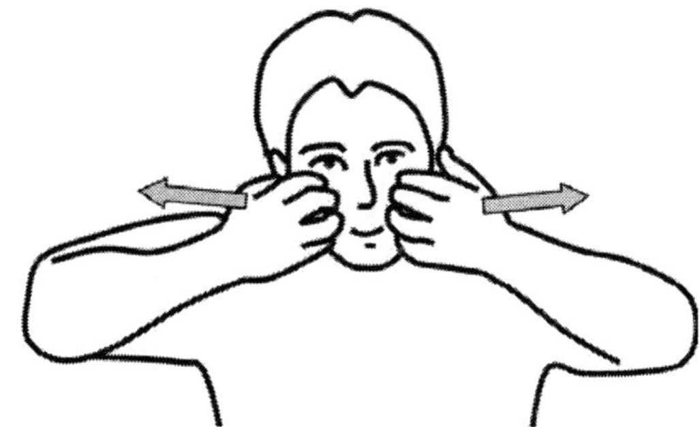
turtle - tortuga Cup the reference palm over the dominant "A" hand and wiggle the dominant thumb with a repeated movement. As if the turtle's head is coming out of its shell.	
worm – gusano, lombriz Make the dominant bent index finger, palm facing forward, make an inch forward against the palm of the reference hand, palm facing right. Indicates a worm inching along.	

afraid - temeroso Begin with the "A" hands on either side of the chest, spread the fingers open with a quick movement changing into "5" hands. [also: scared, frightened, terrified]	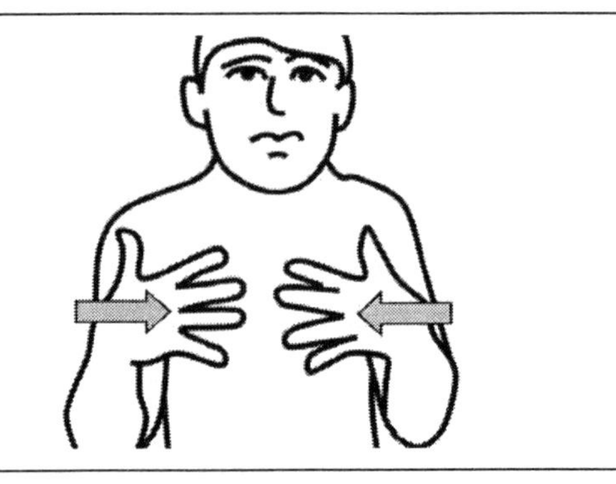
angry – colérico, enojado, enfadado Place the clawed "5" hands against the waist and draw up against the sides of the body. As if anger is boiling up out of person. [also: wrath]	
bored – nade que hacer Place the tip of the index finger against the side of the nose and twist the finger slightly. As if picking one's nose. [also: boring, tedious, dull]	
cry - llorar Draw the index fingers down the cheeks from the eyes several times. [also: weep, tears]	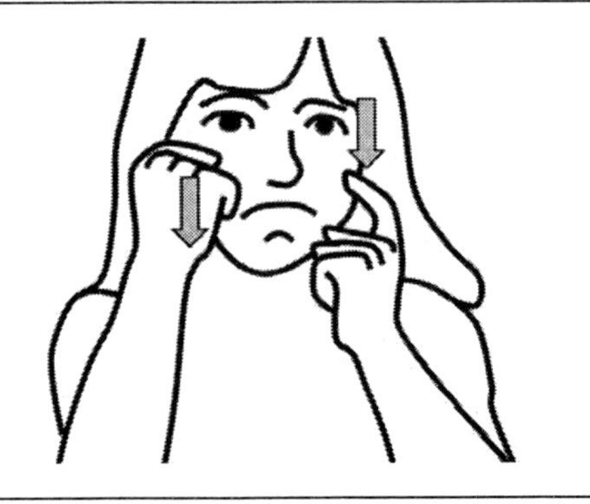

happy- alegre, feliz, contento

The open hands pat the chest several times with a slight upward motion.

As if heart is pounding with joy.

[also, glad, rejoice, joy]

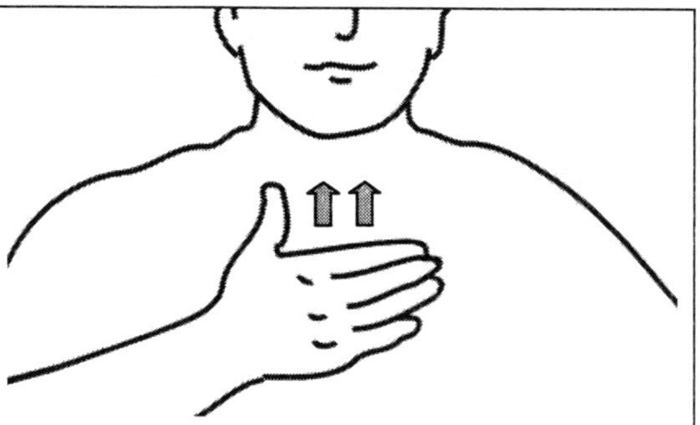

hurt - dolor

The index fingers are moved toward each other several times.

[also: pain, ache]

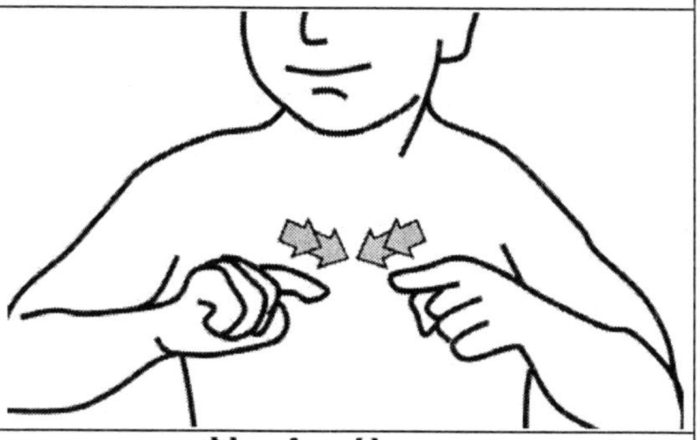

like - gustarle

Place the thumb and the middle finger against the chest (other fingers separated) and draw them away from the body, closing the two fingers.

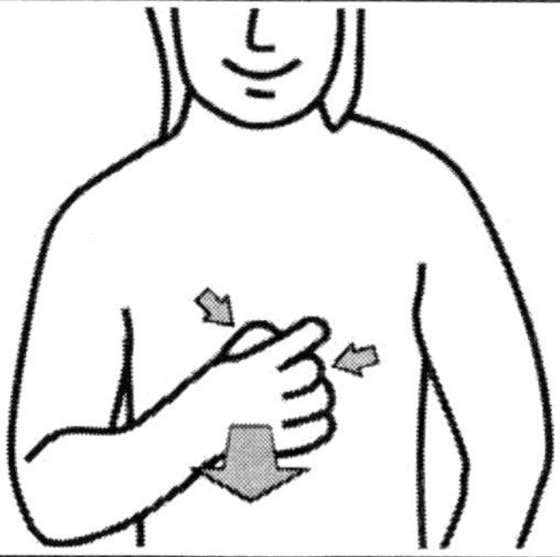

love – amor, cariño

The "S" hands are crossed at the wrist and pressed to the heart.

As if hugging one's self.

patience - paciencia

Place the thumbnail of the dominant hand "A" handshape against the lips and move slowly downward.

[also: endure, bear, suffer]

sad - triste

Hold both open hands in front of the face, fingers slightly apart and pointing up; then drop both hands a short distance and bend the head slightly.

[also: dejected, sorrowful, downcast]

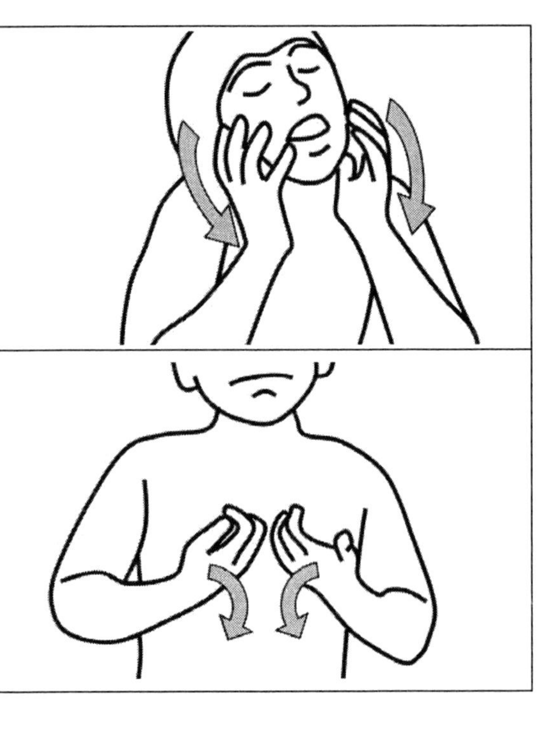

tired – cansado(a)

Fingertips of the bent hands are placed at each side of the body just above the waist and then dropped slightly.

[also: weary, exhausted]

baby – criatura, bebé Place the dominant hand in the crook of the reference hand and make a gentle rocking motion from side to side. As if cradling a baby in your arms.	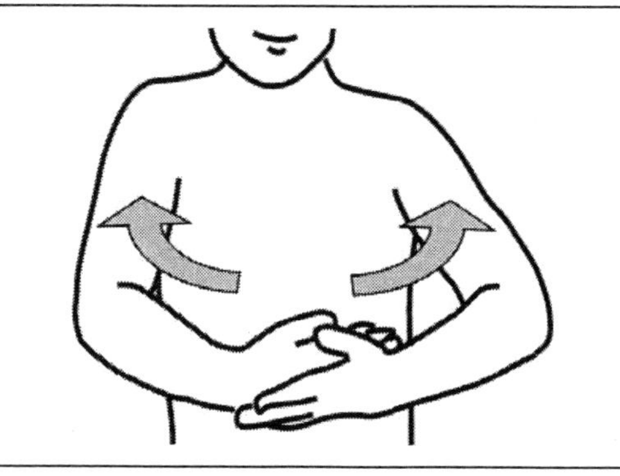
brother - hermano Sign "BOY" and "SAME". First move with the index-finger side of the dominant "C" hand near the dominant side of the forehead, close the fingers to the thumb with a repeated movement. Then place both index fingers side by side, pointing to the front.	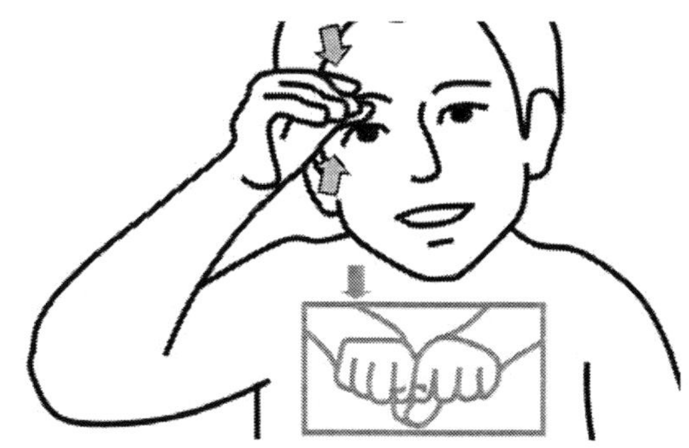
father - padre Place the thumb of the dominant "5" hand on the forehead.	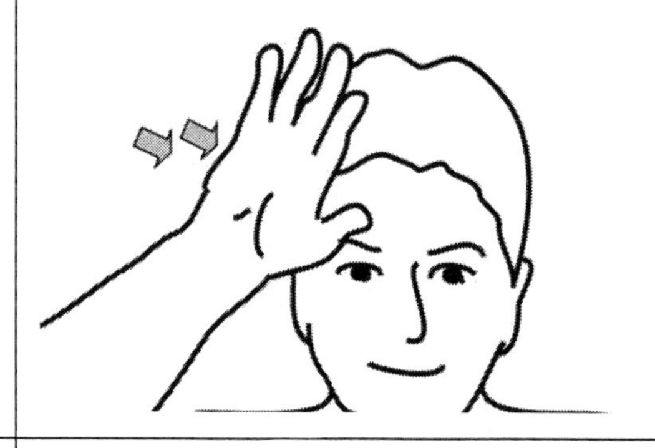
family - familia Place the "F" hands in front of you, palms facing forward; rotate hands apart and away from you; turning until the little fingers touch.	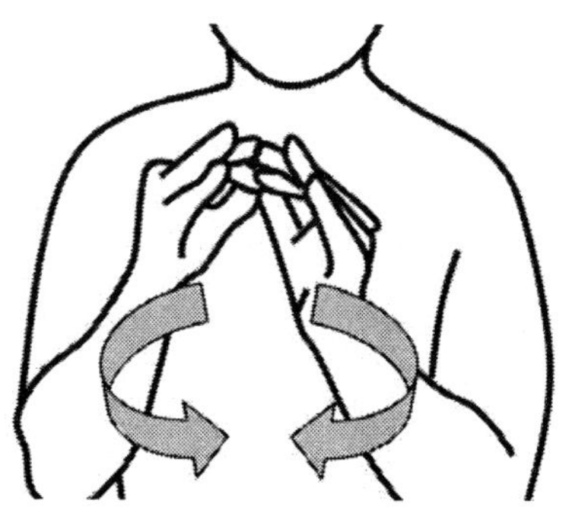

grandfather - abuelo

Sign “father”. Place the thumb of the dominant “5” hand on the forehead, then bounce outward from forehead once.

Origin: One generation away from father.

grandmother - abuela

Sign "mother". Place the thumb of the “5” hand on the chin, then bounce forward once.

Origin: One generation away from mother.

home – hogar, casa

Place the tips of the "flat O" hand against the mouth and then the cheek (or, place the flat hand on the cheek.)

love – amor, cariño

The "S" hands are crossed at the wrist and pressed to the heart.

As if hugging one’s self.

mother - madre

Place the thumb of the “5” hand on the chin.

sister - hermana Sign "GIRL", then "SAME". First move the thumb of the dominant "A" hand, downward on the dominant cheek to the dominant side of the chin. Then place both index fingers side by side, pointing to the front.	

good – bueno(a), bien

Starting with fingertips of the open hand on the lips, move the hand down to touch the open palm.

As if something tasted good and you want more.

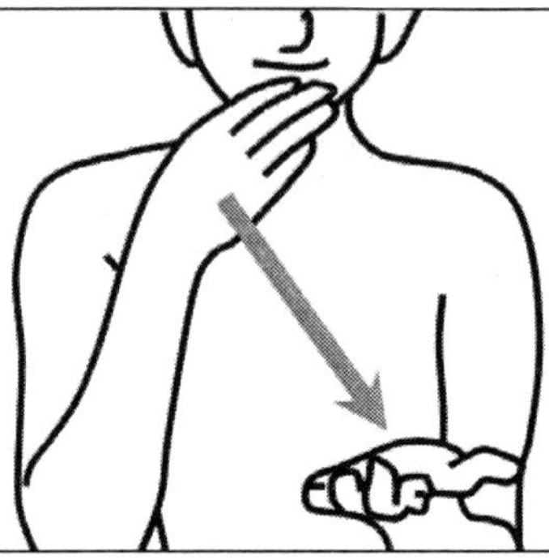

help - ayuda

Place the dominant open hand under the reference "S", thumbs up, lift both hands together.

[also: aid, assist]

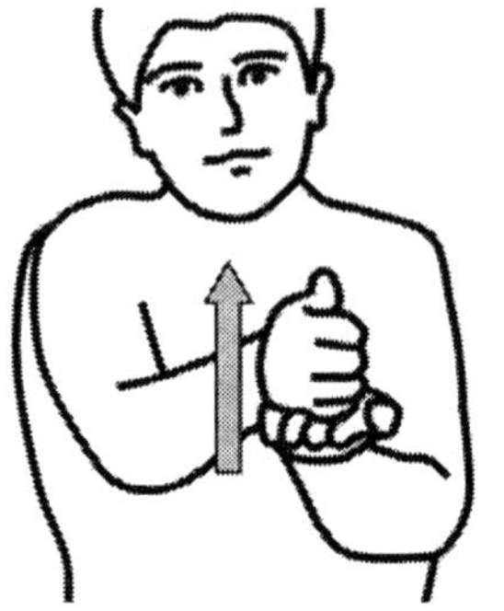

more - más

Bring the tips of both "flat O" hands together, pop together 2 times.

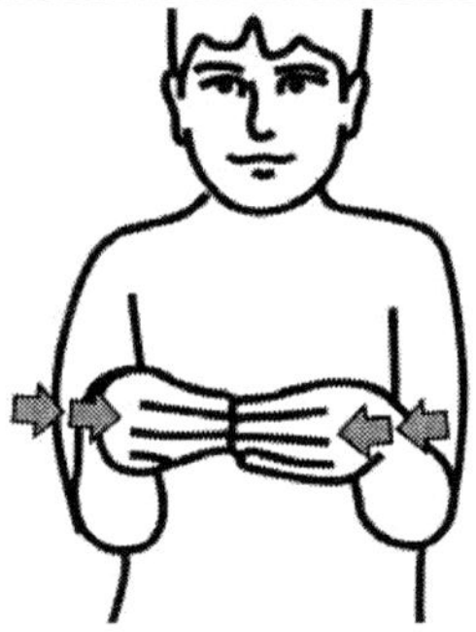

no - no

Bring the index, middle finger, and thumb together in one motion.

please – por favor Rub the chest with the open hand in a circular motion (palm facing yourself) As if rubbing your heart. [also: pleasure, enjoy, like]	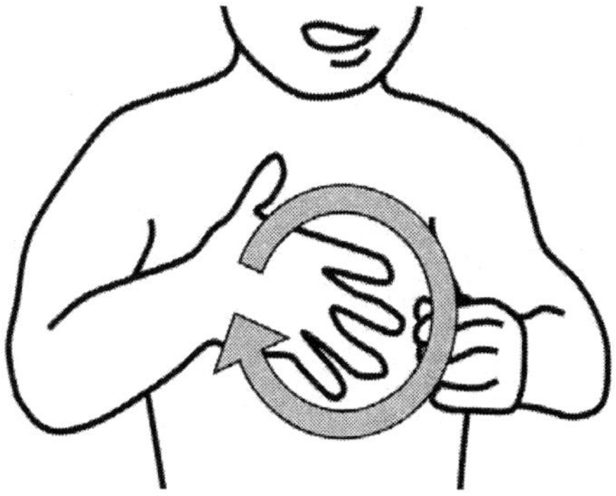
thank you - gracias Touch lips with the fingertips of flat hand, then move the hand forward until the palm is facing up and towards the indicated person. Smile and nod head while doing this sign.	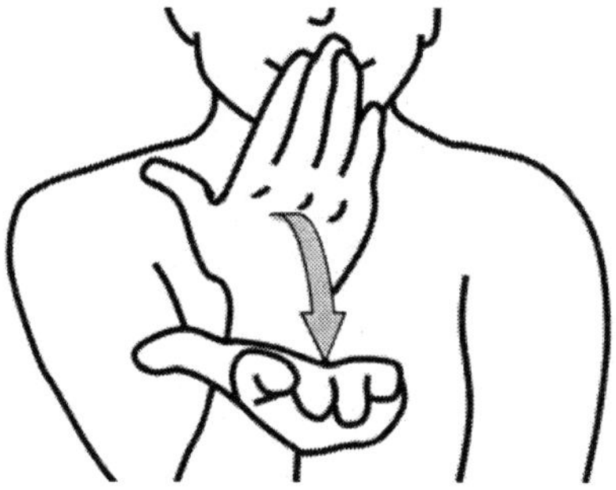
welcome – bienvenido Bring the upturned dominant curved hand from in front of the dominant side of the body in toward the center of the waist. **You are welcome – de nada**	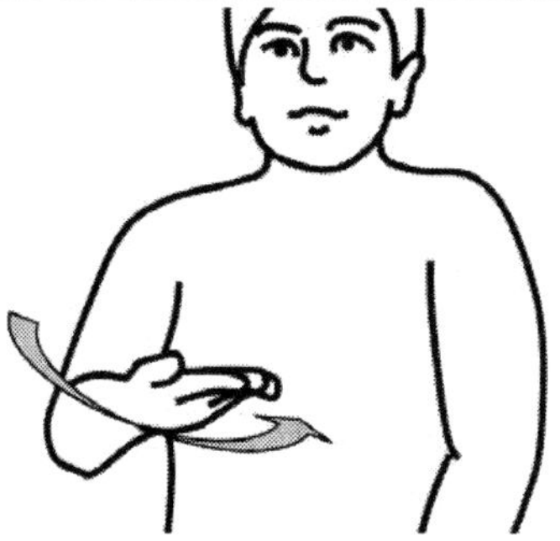
yes - sí Shake the "S" up and down in front of you.	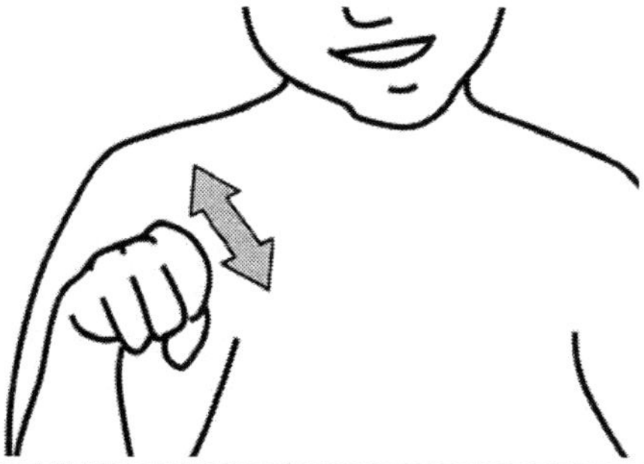

book - libro

Starting with both palms touching in front of the chest, fingers pointing forward, move the hands apart, keeping the little fingers together.

As if opening a book.

bus - autobús

[Initialized sign.]
Beginning with the little-fingers side of the dominant “B” hand touching the index-finger side of the reference “B” hand, palms facing in opposite directions, move the dominant hand back towards the dominant shoulder.

change - cambio

With both modified "X" hands, place the dominant "X" so the palm faces forward, with the reference "X" facing it. Twist the hands around until they have reversed positions.

[also: adjust, adapt]

dance - baile

Place the "V" in the standing position on the reference palm and swing the "V" back and forth as if dancing with the fingers.

friend – amigo(a)

Interlock dominant "X" hand index finger down over upturned reference "X" hand index finger.

As if holding hands with someone.

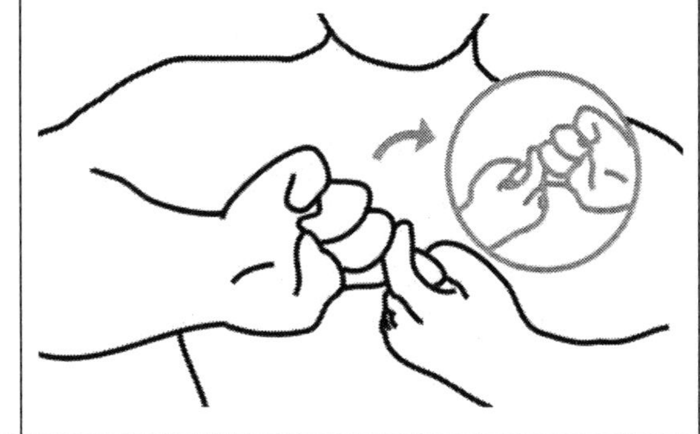

game – juego, jugar

Bring the “A” hands towards each other, palms toward the body, in a slightly upward motion.

As if two people facing each other in competition.

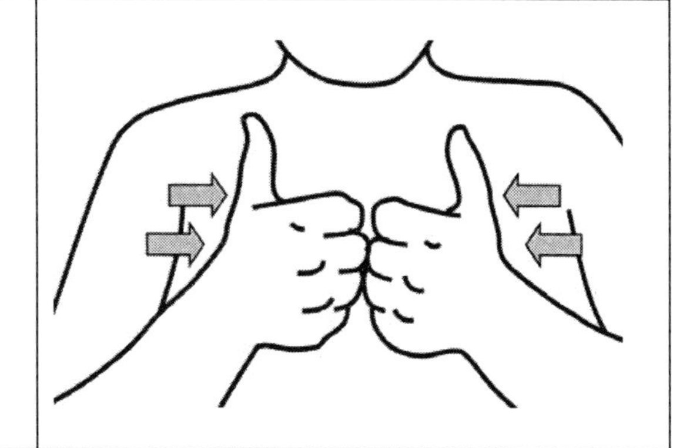

glue – cola para pegar, pega

Move the fingertips of the dominant "G" hand, palm and fingers facing down in a circular movement over the upturned reference open hand.

You can also fingerspell G-L-U-E.

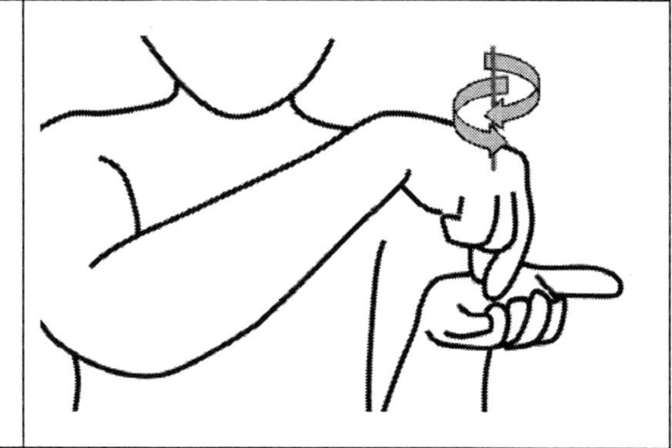

good – bueno(a), bien

Starting with fingertips of the open hand on the lips, move the hand down to touch the open palm.

As if something tasted good and you want more.

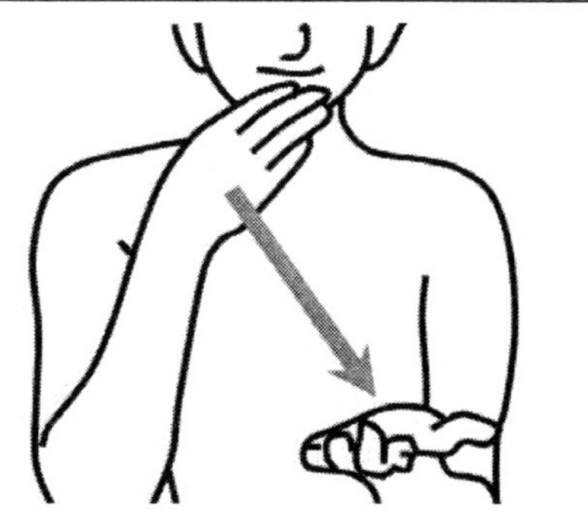

hear – oir, escuchar Point the index finger towards the ear. As if showing the ear to listen. [also: ear]	
help - ayuda Place the dominant open hand under the reference "A" hand, thumb up, lift both hands together. [also: aid, assist]	
paper – papel Sweep the heel of the dominant "5" hand, palm down, back against the heel of the upturned reference "5" hand with an upward motion.	
please – por favor Rub the chest with the open hand in a circular motion (palm facing yourself) As if rubbing your heart. [also: pleasure, enjoy, like]	
quiet – callado, callar, silencio Place the index finger against the mouth. As if to make the "shhh" sound.	

school - escuela Tap the fingers of the dominant open hand, palm facing down, with a double movement of the upturned palm of the reference open hand.	
scissors - tijera [Wrist motion, finger motion] With the "H" hand turned, palm facing self, open and close fingers repeatedly as if your hand was a pair of scissors.	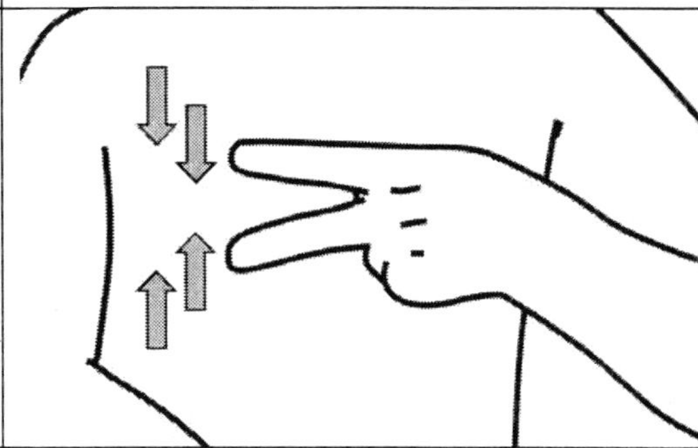
share – compartir, participar Open dominant hand is placed in the crook of the open reference hand and moves back and forth as if cutting a portion of something to share. As if cutting a portion.	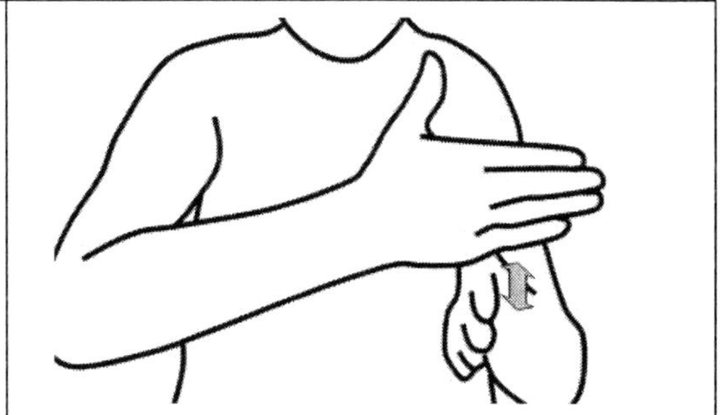
sit - sentarse Place the fingers of the "H" hand on top of the reference "H" hand, palms facing down, as if sitting on a bench. As if two legs are dangling from a bench.	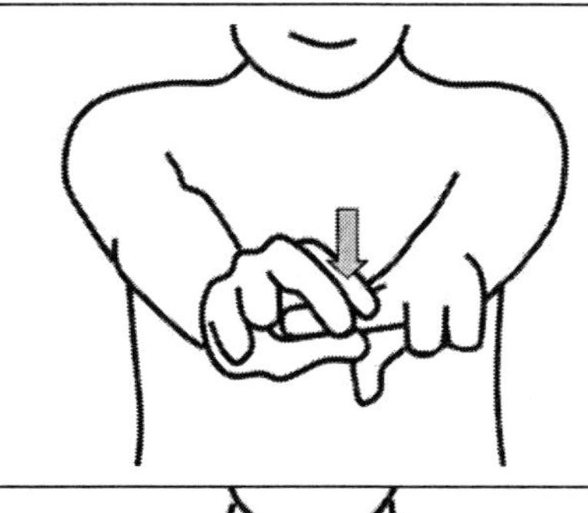
stop – parar, alto, detener, poner fin Bring the little finger side of the dominant open hand abruptly down on the upturned reference palm. As if chopping on something.	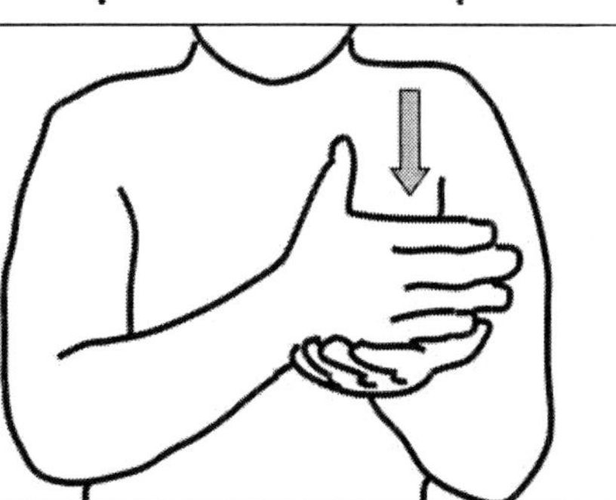

Teacher, teach – maestro(a), enseñar Move both "flattened O" hands, forward with a small double movement in front of each side of the head. Teacher ends with the "er" (person) modifier. The hands seem to take information from the head and direct it to another person.	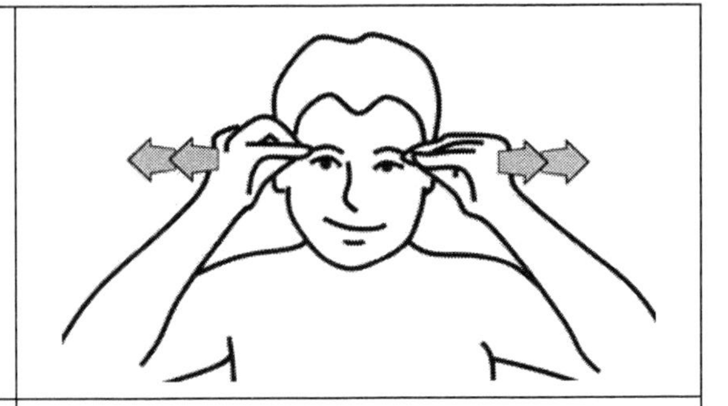
Teacher's Aide – maestro(a) ayudante First move both flattened "O" hands, palms facing each other, forward with a small double movement in front of each side of the head. [The hands seem to take information from the head and direct it from another person.] Then use the thumb of the dominant "A" hand under the little-finger side of the reference "A" hand to push the reference hand upward in front of the chest. [Hands show a boost being given.]	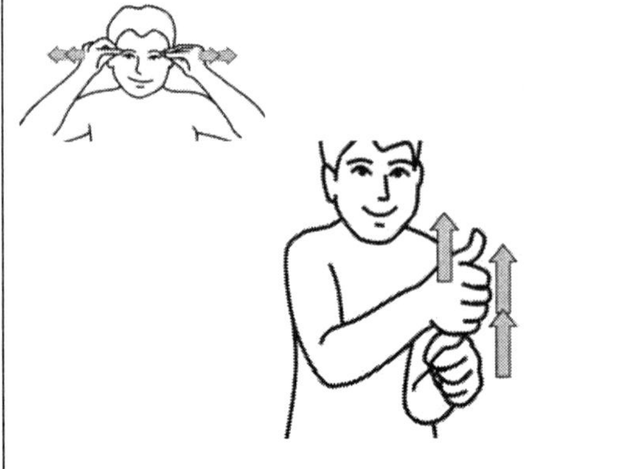
thank you - gracias Touch lips with the fingertips of flat hand, then move the hand forward until the palm is facing up and towards the indicated person. Smile and nod head while doing this sign.	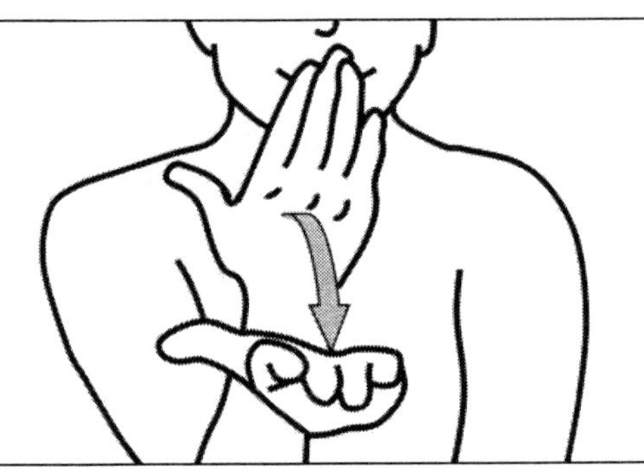
think – pensar, creer Tap the extended dominant index finger to the dominant side of the forehead with a short double movement.	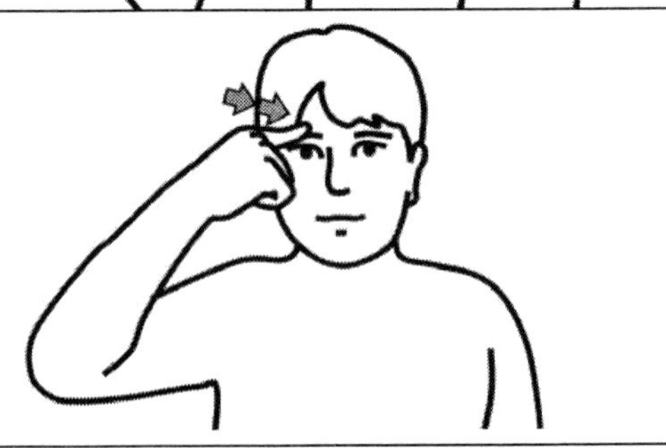
time – tiempo, hora Tap the bent index finger of the dominant "X" hand with a double movement on the wrist of the reference held in front of the chest, palm facing down. As if tapping on a watch.	

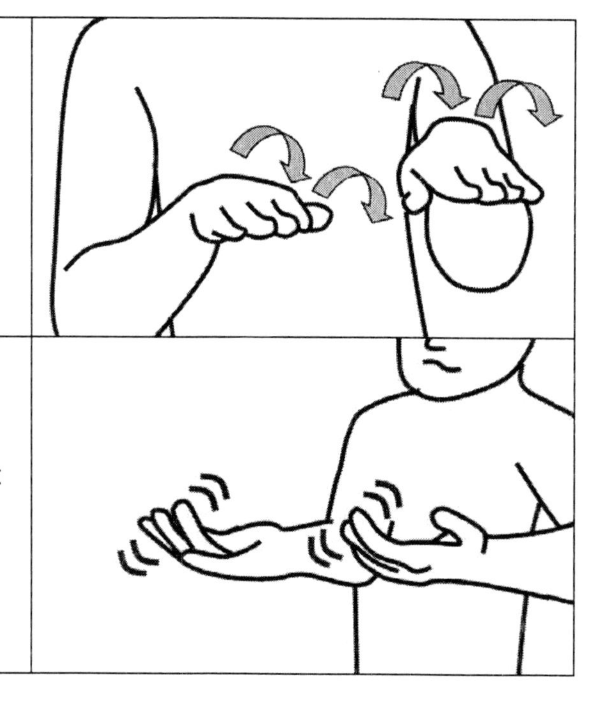

walk – paseo, andar, caminar Open hands, palms down, are moved in a forward-downward motion alternately As if walking with the hands.	
wait – espera, esperar Beginning with both curved "5" hands in front of the body, reference palm up in front of the dominant palm up, wiggle the fingers. As if asking for something.	

Winter - Invierno

Shake both "W" hands, palms facing each other.

Spring - Primavera

The dominant "flat O" hand opens as it comes up through the reference "C".

As if a plant is springing up.

[also: means grow.]

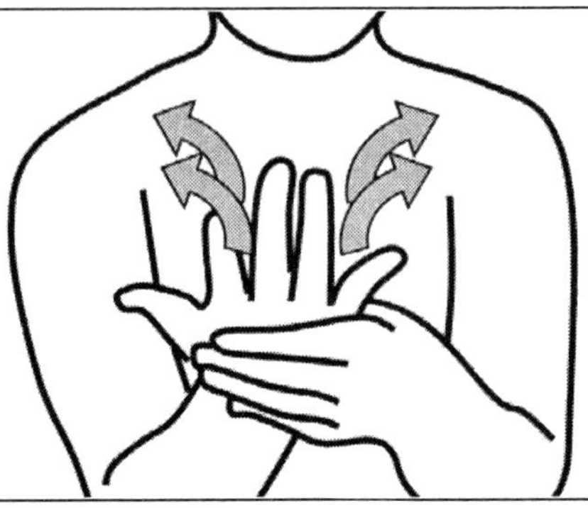

Summer - Verano

The dominant index finger is pointed then crooked as it is wiped across the forehead.

As if wiping sweat from the brow.

Fall, Autumn - Otoño

The reference open hand points upward toward the dominant side. The dominant open hand brushes downward along the reference forearm with the edge of the dominant index finger.

apple - manzana With the knuckle of the bent index finger on the dominant cheek, twist downward.	
banana - plátano Move the closed fingertips of the dominant hand, down the extended reference index finger. As if peeling your index finger.	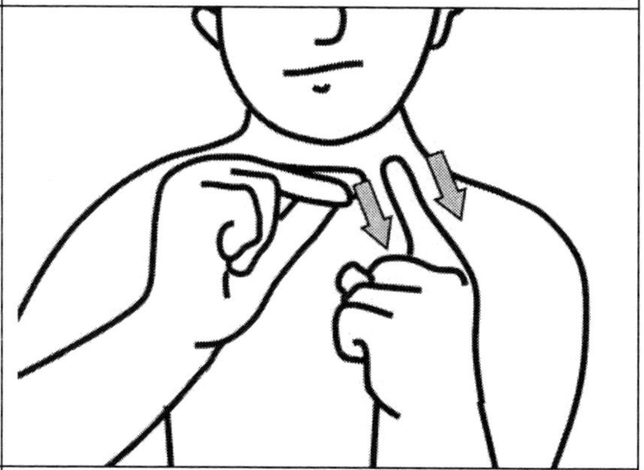
berry - grano Surround the little fingertip of the reference "I" hand, palm toward body, with the dominant fingertips, thumb at the bottom and twist dominant hand away from the body several times. Add signed color of berry to be more specific (Sample - sign blue for blueberry).	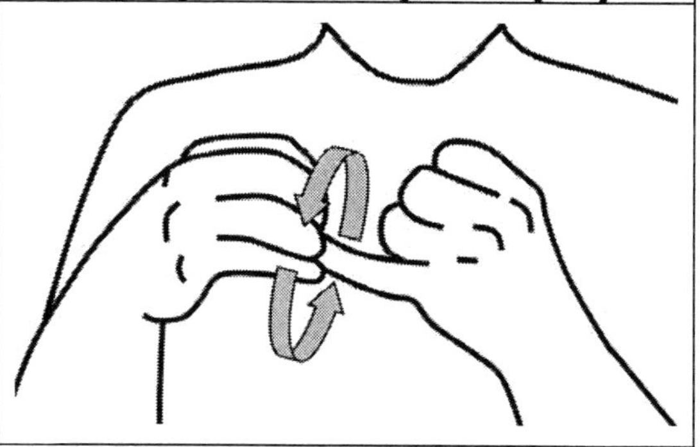
carrot - zanahoria Place the "S" hand near the dominant side of your mouth and move it slowly inward toward the mouth. As if chewing or biting a carrot.	

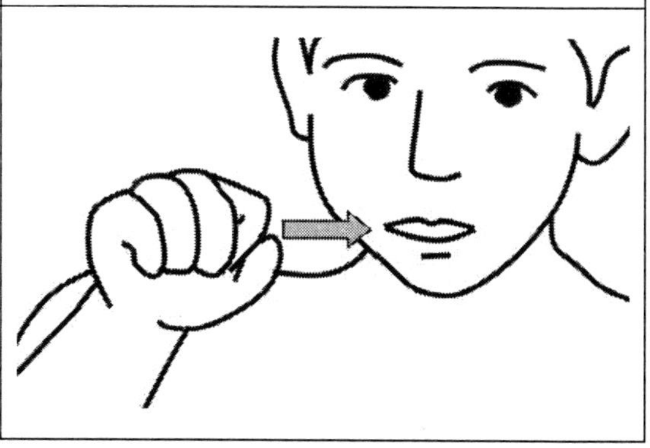

cookie - galleta

Touch the fingers of the dominant clawed "5" hand on the upturned reference palm and then twist the dominant hand and touch the reference palm again.

As if cutting cookies with a cookie cutter.

drink - bebida, tomar, beber

Use the "c" hand in front of the mouth and thumb touching bottom lip; then keeping the thumb in place, move fingers upward toward the nose.

As if taking a drink with the hands.

eat - comer

With the thumb and fingertips together, palm facing down, repeatedly move the fingertips towards the lip with short movements.

As if putting food in ones mouth.

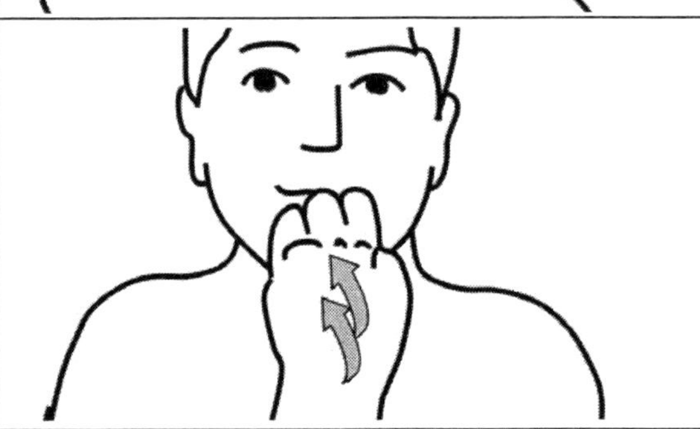

French fry – papas fritas

Make an "F" hand in front of the body, moving hands slightly to the dominant.

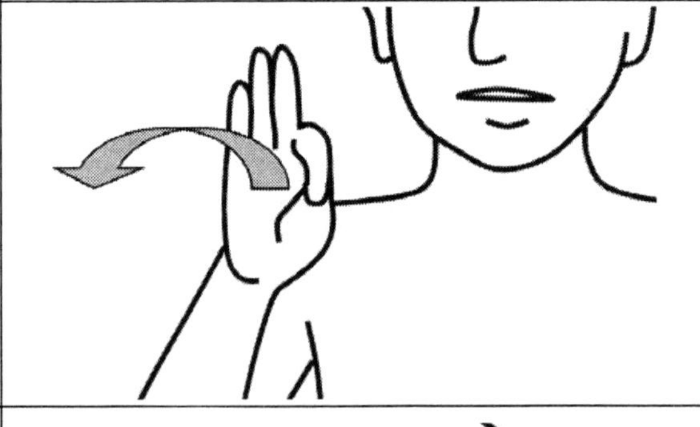

grapes - uvas

Draw the dominant "claw" hand over the back of the open reference hand. Show a bunch of grapes.

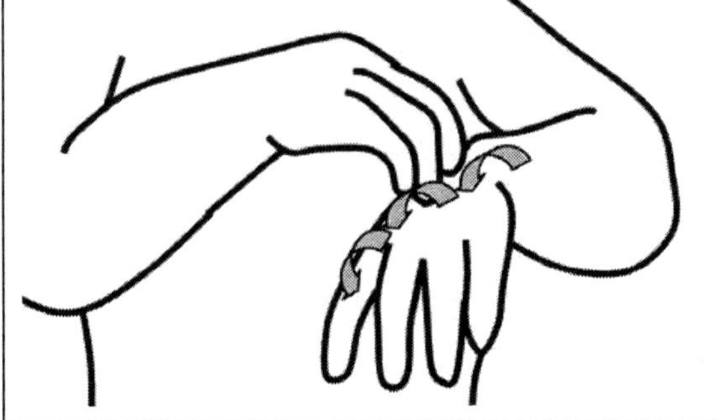

milk - leche

Begin with the "C" hand in front of the body, tighten the hand to an "s" shape, repeatedly.

[As if milking a cow.]

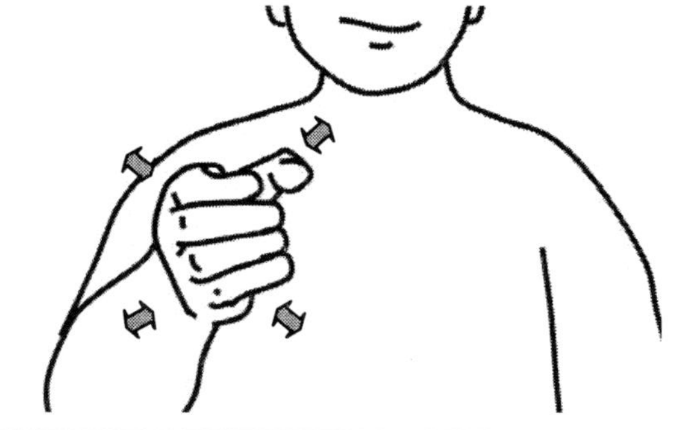

orange – naranja

Squeeze the "S" hand once or twice at the chin. Sign for the color the fruit.

[Same sign for color or fruit]

orange – anaranjado

Squeeze the "S" hand once or twice at the chin. Sign for the color orange.

pizza - pizza

Make a "P" hand in front of your body and then with the "P" hand, draw a "Z."

You can fingerspell P-I-Z-Z-A.

water - agua

Touch the mouth with the index finger of the "W" hand a few times.

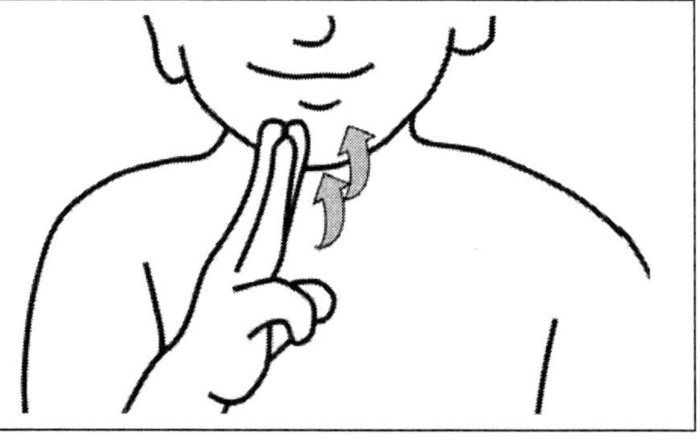

cloud(s) - nube Begin with both "C" hands near the reference side of the head, palms facing each other, bring the hands away from each other in outward arcs while turning the palms in. Repeat near the dominant side of the head. Shape and location of clouds.	
outside – fuera, afuera The dominant open "flat O" hand, facing the body and pointing down, becomes closed as it moves up through the reference "C" hand, which then becomes an "O".	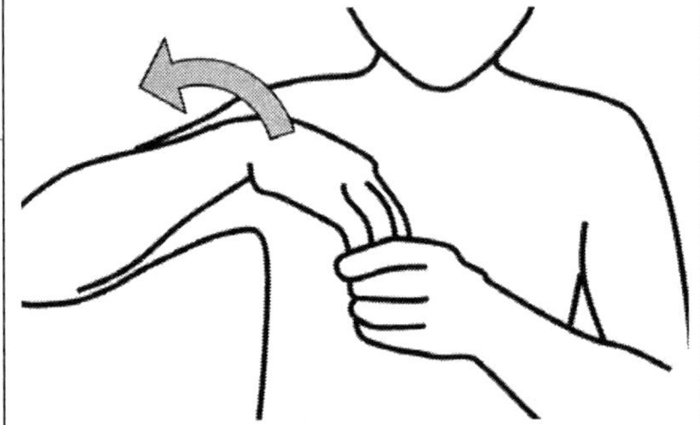
rain - lluvia Let both curved "5" hands, palms facing down, drop down several times in short, quick motions.	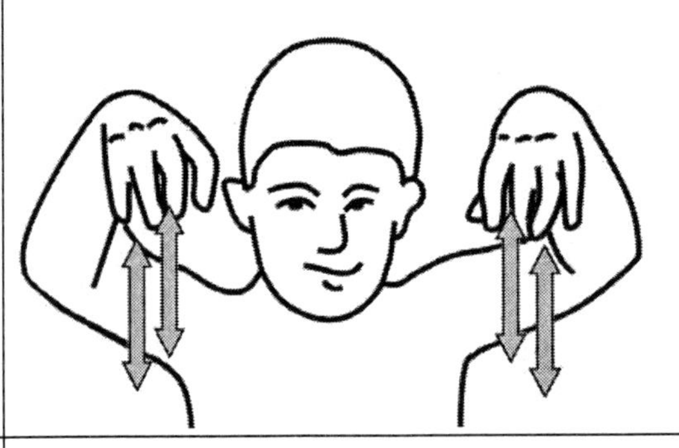
snow - nieve Let both "5" hands, palm down, drop down while gently wiggling the fingers. As if snowflakes pointing downward.	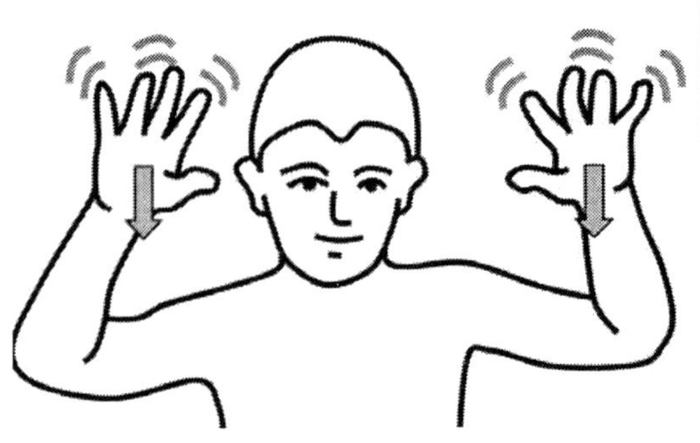

sun - sol The "C"' hand is held at the dominant temple and extended forward and upward.	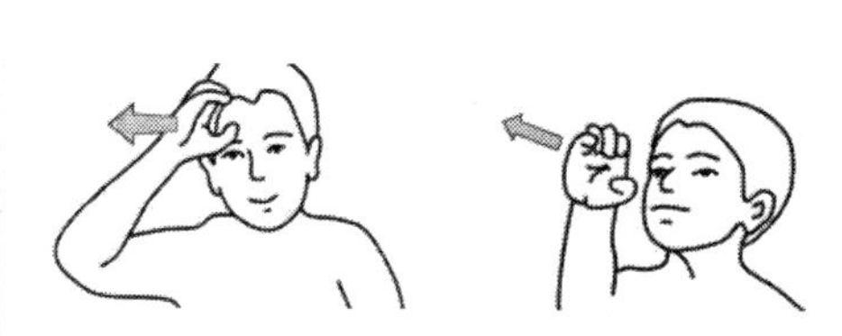
wind - viento Beginning with both "5" hands in front of the reference side of the body, palms facing each other and fingers pointing outward, move the hands back and forth in front of the chest in a repeated movement. Indicates the action of wind blowing.	

Play to Learn!

Play is the work of children. Children enjoy playing. Playing involves creativity and imagination. Children may run, hop, jump, hide, build, paint, read, or write as they play. Play can take place anywhere at any time. Sometimes children create their own rules when they are playing together. They may pretend that their play activities are real. Children are active learners during play.

"Young children do not differentiate between play, learning, and work. When children are engaged in play, they are learning and enjoying every minute of it." Rogers & Sawyers, 1988, p.7

WHY IS PLAY IMPORTANT?

Children explore their world by playing in it. Play gives children an opportunity to practice and develop new skills such as creativity, motor, social, and problem solving. Children can also express their emotions through play. Playing with puppets and other toys can help children share their emotions with their parents and caregivers.

Children are successful when they play because they often choose games and materials that are "just dominant" for them. They are able to decide if activities are too easy or too difficult for them. It is important for adults to praise and encourage children's efforts. Play also gives children a chance to socialize with each other as they experiment (play) with language.

TYPES OF PLAY

Exploratory or Sensorimotor Play

Children create sensations by playing with objects, their actions produce effects that can be observed by the senses. Example: Pouring sand into containers, splashing in puddles, or banging objects together.

Relational or Functional Play

Playing with objects in a realistic way. Example: Using a sponge and hose to wash a car.

Constructive Play

Children show a purpose for using toys and materials to reach a goal. Example: Using a shovel and pail to build a sand castle.

Dramatic or Symbolic Play
Children pretend to be another person or character, they also use objects to stand for other things that aren't in the play area. Examples: A child may pretend to be a character from a book or TV show, and then pretend that their character is at the beach, or fishing with a ruler (fishing pole) at a make believe lake.

Games-with-Rules Play
The players agree to accept rules for their playing, games may include competition with self or others, they may use standard board or card games, or invent their own game. Examples: Children playing Go-Fish. Or children playing a game about a trip to another planet.

Rough and Tumble Play
Players engage in physical contact and are actively involved, this type of play is different from aggressive behavior. Example: Children running, chasing, wrestling, or tickling each other.

TYPES OF PEER PLAY

Unoccupied
Observes others playing but doesn't join them.

Onlooker
Talks with others who are playing to ask questions, observes, but doesn't join them.

Solitary Independent Play
Plays by self near other children, doesn't make contact with them.

Parallel Activity
Plays near other children and uses similar toys and ideas, but doesn't play with the other children.

Associative Play
Shared activities among children who borrow, trade, and share toys, their conversations influence each other's play, they do not have a common goal.

Cooperative or Organized Supplementary Play
Social play, shared goal, continuous interactions, the group may produce dramas by following the instructions of the leader.

(Parten, 1932 as cited in Rogers & Sawyers, 1988)

PLAY: THE FOUNDATION FOR LEARNING

Sociodramatic play is related to literacy. Both activities involve the use of symbols to represent ideas. For example, in sociodramatic play, children may use wooden blocks as trucks. The blocks represent the idea of trucks. Later during reading and writing activities, children will understand that spoken and printed words also stand for ideas and concepts. Caregivers can create learning centers that encourage children to experiment (play) with literacy. By using stories, experience charts, journals, and drawing pictures, teachers and parents can demonstrate the pleasure and function of literacy for children.

THE IMPORTANCE OF PLAYGROUPS FOR YOUNG CHILDREN AND PARENTS

In most playgroups, children and their parents meet on a weekly basis for an hour or two of play and conversation. All members may also share a simple snack and juice during this time together. Playgroups give parents a chance to support and learn from each other. Children gain experiences in sharing, turn taking, and practicing positive social behaviors. Playgroups may be hosted by the parents of children in the group, held at a local library, a neighborhood school, or at a community center.

PLAYGROUP TIPS FOR PARENTS

- Think about your needs and your child's needs. Consider the type of setting that you will both need to feel comfortable with other parents and their children.

- Look for or create a playgroup where all of the children are nearly the same age. These children are likely to share each other's interests and to reach developmental stages at the same time.

- Find a playgroup before you think that you might need outside support for you and your child.

- Be flexible regarding schedules, ideas, and concerns. Follow the children's leads whenever appropriate.

- Develop ground rules before you meet as a group with the kids. Gather now and again to discuss activities, plans, and concerns.

- Before hosting a session, decide where to place toys and other items that are off-limits for your guests, and be sure to ask other parents about food and drink allergies.

- Look for inexpensive toys at garage sales and flea markets. Try to have at least two of each item, this will lead to lessons about sharing.

- Borrow The Playgroup Handbook, by Nancy Towner and Laura Peabody Broad, from your local library. This book contains information about and activities for playgroups.

- Discuss the experiences that you and your child have at playgroup. Remain involved if you are both enjoying yourselves.

RESOURCES

Federal Assistance and Support

Child Care Bureau
U.S. Department of Health and Human Services
Administration for Children and Families
Office of Public Affairs
370 L'Enfant Promenade, S.W.
Washington, D.C. 20202

Corporation for National Service
Training and Technical Assistance
Room 4821
1201 New York Avenue, N.W.
Washington, D.C. 20595

Even Start
U.S. Department of Education
Compensatory Education Programs
Office of Elementary and Secondary Education
600 Independence Avenue, S.W.
Room 4400
Portals Building
Washington, D.C. 20202-6132

Head Start
U.S. Department of Health and Human Services
Administration for Children and Families
Office of Public Affairs
370 L'Enfant Promenade, S.W.
Washington, D.C. 20202

National Information Center for Children and Youth with Disabilities
P.O. Box 1492
Washington, D.C. 20013

National Institute of Child Health and Human Development
U.S. Department of Health and Human Services
National Institutes of Child Health
Building 31, Room 2A32, MSC-2425
31 Center Drive
Bethesda, MD 20842-2425

Office of Special Education Programs
U.S. Department of Education
600 Independence Avenue, S.W.
Switzer Building
Room 4613
Washington, D.C. 20202

Title I
U.S. Department of Education
Compensatory Education programs
Office of Elementary and Secondary Education
600 Independence Avenue, S.W.
Room 4400
Portals Building
Washington, D.C. 20202-6132

American Speech-Language-Hearing Association (ASHA)
10801 Rockville Pike
Rockville, MD 20852
301-897-700 (voice and TTY)
800-638-8255 (toll-free)
Website: http://www.cleft.com

Council for Exceptional Children (CEC)
Division for Children with Communication Disorders
1920 Association Drive
Reston, VA 22091-1589
703-620-3660
Website: http://www.cec.sped.org

Organizations

Alliance for Technology Access
2175 East Francisco Boulevard
Suite L
San Rafael, CA 94901
415-455-4575

Gallaudet University
Washington, D.C.
(800) 526-9105

National Easter Seal Society
230 West Monroe Street
Suite 1800
Chicago, IL 60606-4802
312-726-6200
312-726-4258 (TTY)
Website: http://www.seals.com

Other Resources

Dr. Marilyn Daniels
Associate Professor
Department of Speech Communication
Penn State University
120 Ridge View Drive
Dunmore, PA 18512-1699
Office 570 963-2670
FAX 570 963-2535
Mail to:mxd34@psu.edu

Garlic Press
www.garlicpress.com
Sign Language Books and Materials

Kathy & Tom
www.kathyandtom.com
Music for Children

Odd Man Out
Mary Miller (321) 952-1994
Music for Children and Christian Music

Telephone Help

Ultratec, Inc. (TTY)
450 Science Drive
Madison, WI 53711
U.S.A.
(608) 238-5400 PHONE
(608) 238-3008 FAX
Website: www.ultratec.com

Child Care Aware
800-424-2246 (toll free)
Referrals to licenses and accredited childcare centers. Also provides a free packet of information on how to choose quality childcare. Coordinated by the National Association of Child Care Resource and Referral Agencies.
Weekdays, 9:00 a.m. – 5:00 p.m. (CST)

Child Help National Hotline
800-443-7237
Twenty-four hour advice and referrals for children and adults with questions or in a crisis.

National Parent Information Network
800-583-4135
Referrals, abstracts, and answers from researchers free of charge
Weekdays, 8:00 a.m. – 4:30 p.m. (PST)

Single Parents Association
800-704-2102
Referrals to local support groups and community resources. Also, fields questions on parenting skills.
Weekdays, 9:00 a.m. – 6:00 p.m. (CST)

Websites

Childbirth.Org
http://www.childbirth.org
Top discussion forums and a home page with answers to tough questions

Family.com
http://www.family.com
A Disney site. Bulletin board and chat rooms with voices of intelligent and caring parents.

http://www.geocities.com/babysigning
A guide for parents interested in signing with their babies.

http://www.handspeak.com
Dictionary lets users look up more than 2,800 signs, including common signs for babies.

http://www.masterstech-home/ASLDict.html
Has fewer signs that Handspeak.com but uses animation to help people learn signs.

Parent Talk Newsletter
http://www.tnpc.com/parentalk/index.html
Clearly written articles by physicians and psychologists.

Parenthood Web
http://parenthoodweb.com

Parenting Q&A
http://parenting-qa.com

Zero toThree
http://www.zerotothree.org

REFERENCES

Daniels, Dr. Marilyn (2000). Dancing with Words: Signing for Hearing Children's Literacy. Westport, CT: Bergin & Garvey.

Chambers, Diane P. (1998). Communicating in Sign: Creative Ways to Learn American Sign Language (ASL). New York: Fireside.

Dougherty, Dorothy P. (1999). How to Talk to Your Baby. New York: Avery.

Garcia, Joseph. (1999). Sign With Your Baby: How to communicate with infants before they can speak. Seattle, WA: Northlight Communications.

References for Incorporating Signing into Your Daily Routine

Bonvillian, J. D., Orlansky, M. D., & Novack, L. L. (1983). Developmental milestones: Sign language acquisition and motor development. Child Development, 54, 1435-1445.

Conflitti, C. (1998, February). Early Cognitive Development and American Sign Language. Exceptional Parent, 40-41.

Cutting, J. E. (1980). Sign Language and Spoken Language. Nature, 284, 661-662

Davis, L. (2000, January). Searching for sign, the language of home. The Chronicle of Higher Education, B4-B5.

Drasgow, E. (1998). American Sign Language as a Pathway to Linguistic Competence. Exceptional Children 64 (3), 329-342. Available at http://proquest.umi.com.

Felzer, L. (1998). A Multisensory Reading Program that Really Works. Teaching and Change, 5 (2), 169-183.

Hall, S. S. & Weatherly, K. S. (1989). Using Sign Language with Tracheotomized Infants and Children. Pediatric Nursing, 15 (4), 362-367.

Raimondo, B. (2000). Perspective. Infants and Young Children, 12 (4), 4-7.

Signs of Success (1999). Reading Today 16 (5), 14-15.

References for Development Milestones Section

Brazelton, T. Berry. (1992). Touchpoints: Your child's emotional and behavioral development. Reading, MA: Addison-Wesley Publishing Company.

Gard, Gillman & Gorman. (1993). Speech and Language Milestones.

Reese, Debbie. (June, 1998). Development in Infant and Toddler Speech.

Shelov, Stephen P. (1994). The American Academy of Pediatrics: Caring for your baby and young child. New York: Bantam Books.

SPECIAL THANKS
Gregory H. Chenault, Drawing Illustrator.
Brian Miller, Drawing Illustrator.
Alicia Thoennes, Manual Contributor, Play Section.
Marty Windham, ASAP Printing & Mailing, (703) 836-2288, Publishing.